THE *Gift* OF
HOSPITALITY

THE *Gift* OF
HOSPITALITY

In Church · In the Home
In All of Life

DELIA HALVERSON

Chalice Press
St. Louis, Missouri

Cover: Wendy Barnes
Interior design: Elizabeth Wright
Art Director: Elizabeth Wright

This book is printed on acid-free, recycled paper.

Visit Chalice Press on the World Wide Web at
www.chalicepress.com

10 9 8 7 6 5 4 3 2 1   99 00 01 02 03 04

Library of Congress Cataloging–in–Publication Data

Halverson, Delia Touchton.
    The gift of hospitality : in church, in the home, in all of life / by Delia Halverson.
       p.   cm.
    ISBN 0-8272-1243-7
    1. Hospitality–Religious aspects–Christianity.   I. Title.
BV4647.H67H36 1999
241'.671 – dc21   99-43442
                                                                                          CIP

Printed in the United States of America

To my parents,
Edith and Paul Touchton,
who created a truly welcome and caring space
for anyone in need of love.

Contents

Introduction

Growing up in a parsonage, I never had the experience of searching for a church home. Wherever the bishop sent us was our church home. Then while our family was young, my husband and I lived in towns with a population of 2,000 or less. There was little choice of churches there. And so a move to metropolitan Atlanta was the first opportunity I had to really search for a church home.

This experience brought a new dimension to my understanding of hospitality. As I drove around the neighborhood and observed the churches, I was surprised at what drew me to particular churches. I noticed the pride that was evident in a church's grounds and buildings more than the size of the facility. I realized that I was attracted to a church that had cars in the parking lot at various times throughout the week, because I knew that things were happening in that church, things that might be of interest to me. When attending a service, we were appreciative of the welcoming atmosphere and the way that a bulletin and list of announcements made it easy for us to understand what was going on in the service and to know whether an upcoming activity was something of interest for our family.

We visited one church that appeared to be bursting at the seams with people, but when we walked into the sanctuary a little early for the service we discovered a Sunday school class in session. We had already entered and seated ourselves at the back when we recognized that the class was in serious study. We had no problem with the class meeting in the sanctuary, but we did not appreciate the looks of intrusion that we received from the class members. We tried to make ourselves unobtrusive, but the class was so obviously a cliquish group that they appeared to be centered only on themselves. I'm sure that these folks did not realize the impression they were giving a stranger, but there might have been other options. An usher might have been assigned to the narthex asking newcomers to wait outside until the close of the class session, or a class with a less intensive and more welcoming type of study might have been assigned to meet in the sanctuary, where visitors are apt to appear.

Although this book primarily deals with hospitality in the church, we cannot have a hospitable lifestyle without it spilling over into the home.

A few years ago, when my husband and I were contemplating the purchase of a new home, I had a conversation with a neighbor. I told her of the many neighborhoods in which we had searched for homes. We wanted a friendly neighborhood and the right size house. She suggested a particular house that was on the market, and I told her that it was not large enough. "Not large enough?" she responded. "With just the two of you, why do you want anything more than a one bedroom home? If you only have one bedroom, then your guests will have to stay in a motel, and they won't stay as long."

If you agree with my neighbor, then this book is not for you. If, however, you enjoy having your friends around you, and you thrive on relationships, then read on. Hospitality must come from the heart, and the heart is where the home is.

This book, however, is not just about hospitality in the church and the home. It is about practicing hospitality in all parts of our lives, at home, at work, in the church, and even as we drive to the grocery store.

So why a book on hospitality? Since before Emily Post, we have been confronted with writings suggesting ways that we should act. I recall as a child being intrigued with the guidelines set out by Emily Post, the guru of that era on the proper way to act in order to be accepted in this world. Then came my teen years and early twenties, when I didn't want anyone to tell me how to act, particularly someone I didn't know.

This is not an ordinary book about manners and acts that gain approval. In this book we will recognize hospitality as a gift from God. We will look at various models of hospitality in the Bible as well as ways that Jesus modeled the development of this gift. We will also explore ways that you would like to be treated, as a guideline for acts of hospitality.

The litanies in chapter 8 may be reproduced for occasions of worship; please list this book and its author and publisher as the source.

CHAPTER 1

Gift from Birth

God said, "Now we will make humans, and they will
be like us."

Genesis 1:26a (Contemporary English Version [CEV])

Until we're taught differently, hospitality comes as
a natural instinct. Have you ever watched the reaction
of a six- or twelve-month-old child when given something? The child will perhaps enjoy the gift briefly, but
then he or she will give the gift back to you, with a smile
and possibly a hug to boot. Very early on, however, we
begin to train the natural instinct of hospitality out of
our children. We're told that the "me-ism" of two-year-
olds is typical and important for the child's development.
There is truth in this, but I strongly believe that we push
such actions on the child earlier than necessary, and we
encourage it for far longer than is necessary under the
guise of developing self-esteem.

Just recently when I was waiting to board an airplane, I overheard a mother tell her eighteen-month-old son, "Always take money when it's offered to you!" How early we learn that money and what it can buy are the most important things in the world. This concept is nurtured throughout our lives, as we move from the big wheels of little-kid toys to the even bigger wheels of big-kid toys, always grasping for the height of our credit limits. We even boast about it with bumper stickers: "The one who dies with the most toys wins" or "I'm spending my kid's inheritance." All of life is centered on spending, spending, and spending. With such modeling, how can we expect our children to grow up confirming hospitality?

Personalities and Hospitality

We are all born with the gift of hospitality, even though some personalities find it easier to develop the gift than others. In order to recognize this, let's take a look at the different personality types identified in the Myers-Briggs test.

The first section of the Myers-Briggs personality identity has to do with where we get our energy or how we are revitalized. This is indicated with an E (Extrovert) or I (Introvert). Extroverts get their energy from other people and are, therefore, more inclined to reach out to others. An introvert, however, usually needs to make a conscious decision to create opportunities to practice hospitality. The introvert may resolutely set up events or situations and then have second thoughts as the time arrives. This is a legitimate reaction for introverts. However, by pushing their exposure from time to time, introverts will strengthen their gift of hospitality.

The Myers-Briggs indicator considers the way that we take in information as the second identification of our personality. This is indicated with an S (Sensing) or an N (iNtuitive). Sensers probably find it easier to recognize opportunities for hospitality and to act on those opportunities than intuitives, since intuitives enjoy thoughts more than actions. The intuitive may *intend* to write a thank you note but never get around to it. The senser is more prompted to action. The senser also has a more attuned eye to detail, thereby recognizing things that can make a difference in how others will feel welcomed as they approach a person or a situation. For example, an intuitive may pass the church sign five times a day and not recognize that it has become faded and dull, where a senser will not only recognize that it has lost its luster, but will also probably work on doing something about it. This does not mean that the intuitive cannot be hospitable, only that he or she must make a concentrated effort to recognize ways to practice hospitality.

The third identifying section of the Myers-Briggs test indicates ways that we make decisions. These two choices are identified with an F (Feeling) and a T (Thinking). The thinker is very logical and reasoning when making decisions. He or she looks at a situation and makes a decision, letting the chips fall where they may. On the other hand, the feeling person will be more inclined to avoid conflict and promote harmony. The end result is important to the feeling person. Being more tenderhearted, the feeling personality sees things from the inside, quite naturally thinking about how the other person feels. Since the thinker sees things from the outside, that person looks at the basic facts and fairness of the situation, not being as aware of individuals. Here again, this only indicates that the thinker must make an effort to "walk in another's moccasins" from time to time.

The way that we organize life comes into play with the fourth section of the Myers-Briggs personality profile. This section is indicated with a J (Judger) and a P (Perceiver). Judgers are very precise in plans and decisions. They make lists and enjoy organizing things, delighting in accomplishment. The perceivers tend to be more spontaneous and are always prepared to change their minds. Either of these profile types enables hospitality, but in different ways. The precision and lists of the judger enables plans to run smoothly, which is a definite plus in hospitality. However, the perceiver's ability to act spontaneously and not be upset by changes puts folks at ease and creates a relaxed atmosphere. The judger can disturb others if he or she gets upset when plans and lists do not fall into place. And the obvious lack of preparation on the part of a perceiver can cause folks to feel unimportant and frustrated.

With this understanding of personality, it appears that persons with ESFJ or ESFP personality types will find it easier to be hospitable. However, that does not mean that the rest of us don't have the gift of hospitality. It only means that we must work a little harder in certain areas to develop that gift.

One area that I must constantly bolster myself is in sensing. Too often I look at the whole picture (intuitive) and ignore the details. I have to train myself to pay attention to and appreciate the details. As I travel around the country conducting workshops, I stay in numerous homes. In the past year as I've prepared for this book I have recognized that I've had the most pleasant stays in the homes where I've found the little details attended to, in a quiet, but not fussy sort of way. An example of this is a clear counter in the bathroom where I can lay out my toothbrush and other articles, a nightlight, and a clean glass for water to take my medication. Minor items, but they mean a lot when I'm tired and ready to prepare for bed. Consequently, my guest bathroom at home is now rather sparsely decorated. It also makes cleaning a lot easier when I have very little to clean around!

Recently I had occasion to visit a church not far from my home for a district conference. When I sat down, I saw a box of tissues under the pew in front of me. I assumed it belonged to the person sitting there. In the course of the evening we moved to the fellowship hall for supper and returned to the sanctuary, where I sat in a different area of the room. To my surprise there was again a box of tissues under the pew in front of me. I looked around and realized that tissues were placed near the aisle under each pew. I thought to myself, how hospitable of this church to make tissues so convenient.

In later chapters, we will deal with more specific ways to show hospitality in the church and at home.

CHAPTER 2

Biblical Models of Hospitality

You have heard people say, "Love your neighbors and hate
your enemies." But I tell you to love your enemies and
pray for anyone who mistreats you.

Matthew 5:43–44 (CEV)

Hospitality has been interpreted in many ways, but I feel that true hospitality comes from the heart without expectation of anything in return. As I began to research this subject I made a trip to the public library. To my astonishment, the only listings under hospitality were references to the "hospitality industry" or to such careers as hotel and resort management. This is certainly not my understanding of hospitality. This type of hospitality definitely looks for something in return. I would hope that persons in the hotel and resort management field would act hospitably, but it is not genuine if done only with the ultimate goal of gaining profit.

There are biblical models of hospitality that unmistakably fall into that category. In the twentieth chapter of Genesis, Abraham told everyone that Sarah was his sister (which, although she was his half-sister, still stretched the truth, for she was also his wife). After King Abimelech took Sarah into his household, God came to the king in a dream and explained the situation. In an effort to set things straight with Abraham, and probably in an effort to appease God, the king gave Abraham some sheep, cattle, slaves, and a thousand pieces of silver. This is a type of boomerang hospitality. It comes to a person in response to something that happened before, not as an extension of God's love with no strings attached.

Later in the Bible, however, we have another act toward Abraham that seems to be closer to true hospitality. After Sarah's death, Abraham tried to purchase a cave in which to bury her body (Genesis 23). Before Abraham could even make an offer, Ephron, whom apparently Abraham hardly knew, gave the property to him, insisting that there be no charge. Abraham did pay Ephron for the property in the end, but the act of hospitality was openly offered. This brings to mind the other offer of a tomb made by Joseph of Arimathea after Jesus' death (Matthew 27:57–60; Mark 15:42–46; Luke 23:50–54; John 19:38–42). That was certainly a gift of hospitality that might have brought grave danger to Joseph.

When I searched the internet for biblical bases for hospitality, one of the suggested scriptures was Genesis 19, because Lot offered hospitality to two men (who were angels) in the city of Sodom. I considered not including this scripture as a reference, because in Jewish tradition hospitality was of such great importance that, in order to extend hospitality to the men, Lot offered his two daughters up for rape. In reflection on this, I find an added dimension to the meaning of hospitality. Hospitality to one must not be harmful to another. We may, and often do, suffer inconvenience for the sake of hospitality, but we should never allow it to cause harm.

If we look at hospitality as simply opening our home and table to others, then Jethro's sharing a meal with Moses (Exodus 2:20) would be considered an example of hospitality. I feel, however, that the action of Moses preceding that meal is even more hospitable in character. He helped Jethro's daughters when they had difficulty watering their animals. Assisting women was not considered a chivalrous act in biblical times. As a stranger in the land, Moses could easily have stood by without offering to help. It certainly was not expected of him. That act was hospitality from a man who ventured to step across the lines drawn by culture. By today's standards, Moses might have been considered homeless, for he didn't even own a home to offer. Hospitality is a lifestyle rather than an act of culture.

True hospitality shines through, even in the midst of fear. In Joshua 2:1–16 we read of Rahab, a woman who overcame fear and offered her home to the Hebrew spies. Several people showed hospitality to Jesus, even when the rulers of the day opposed him. One of the primary examples of hospitality in the face of fear is Ananias' welcome to Saul in Acts 9:1–18. Saul was known as a persecutor of the Christians. Where he went, followers of Christ were soon imprisoned, and many were killed. Imagine the fear that must have gripped Ananias when he heard that Saul was in town, and particularly when God told him to go to Saul and welcome him. Without that hospitality from Ananias, Saul might never have become Paul, and without Paul's zeal it may have taken longer for the gospel to spread among the Gentiles.

Martha's hospitality is sometimes evaded because of Jesus' statement about Mary choosing the better thing, recorded in Luke 10:38–42. However, when this story is seen in the culture of the day, we realize that Jesus was not so much condemning Martha's attitude about hospitality as he was claiming the right for women to discuss theology. A woman of that era was never included in theological discussions. She was simply expected to perform household duties and otherwise stay in the background. Jesus' affirmation of Mary's choice was a radical statement for women. It was also an act of hospitality on the part of Jesus, suggesting that Martha sit and soak up the theological discussion that normally would have been denied her.

Jesus would not have returned to the home of Martha and Mary had they not both had the gift of hospitality. The traditional interpretation of the Martha and Mary story has caused us to put spirituality and hospitality in separate, conflicting boxes. In reality, true hospitality cannot come about without some depth of spirituality. And spirituality reaps the fruit of hospitality, because if we truly have Christ in our hearts, we simply must shower that love on others. We must pull these concepts out of their boxes and appreciate the way that they complement each other.

CHAPTER 3

Hospitality of Welcoming

Be sure to welcome strangers into your home. By doing this, some people have welcomed angels as guests,without even knowing it.

Hebrews 13:2 (CEV)

As I clipped tree branches that hung out over the entrance to my home, I wondered what welcome message my doorway sent to those approaching it. I stepped back and tried to see it through the eyes of someone coming into my home. The small potted tree gave the entrance life, as did the smaller potted plant beside the tree. There was a wreath on the door and a welcome sign beside the door. We had purposefully chosen a house that was low to the ground for better access, but there was one step up. A ramp and a wider door would have made it more accessible for physically challenged persons, and a lever door latch instead of a knob would have helped anyone with their arms full. I could not easily replace the door or add a ramp, but I did consider a new door latch.

In Our Daily Lives

One of my favorite books is an African tale of two daughters. John Steptoe has written and illustrated an English version of the tale, *Mufaro's Beautiful Daughters* (published by Lothrop, Lee & Shepard in 1987). The story tells of two daughters who were both beautiful. Manyara was unhappy and resentful, but Nyasha was kind and loving. When the Great King wanted a wife, the father and daughters began the journey to the city so that the girls might be among those considered to be queen. Manyara sneaked out during the night in order to be the first to appear before the king. As she made the journey, she showed no respect for the animals or persons that she met along the way. However, when Nyasha came along the next day, she took the time to stop and care for those she encountered. At the end of the tale we learn that the king himself was each of the animals and persons that Manyara had passed and that Nyasha had comforted. The king chose Nyasha because she treated him with kindness by acting in a kind manner to those she met along the way. Although this story does not have a single "religious" word in it, behind the story line you will recognize Jesus' statement, "as you did it to one of the least of these..." (Matthew 25:40b).

When have we failed to recognize Christ in our everyday lives? Hospitality is recognizing Christ in everyone we meet and acting accordingly.

In the country of Zaire there is a special cloth that is placed on the table when company is coming. This custom gives a signal that something special is about to happen. Someone is coming into the home. We can welcome others into our home with dignity, and it does not need to be elaborate.

For three years I have led a Bible study in our home. The first year we began meeting at the church. At Christmas I invited the group to come to our home for one of the sessions so that I might share our collection of nativity sets. They enjoyed the setting so much that meeting in our home has become a tradition. Every year, our first session starts in the kitchen. There I show them where the cups and glasses are kept. I explain that our way of welcoming them into our home is to allow them to feel at home, and they are welcome to serve themselves coffee, tea, or sodas at any time. This not only puts them at ease, but it also frees me up to extend my hospitality beyond pouring coffee and filling glasses with ice. I also find that I can be more hospitable if I am not in a frenzy over caring for each person's personal needs.

On the other hand, there are times when a person needs some specific caring. I recall some years ago when I was having a particularly stressful time. One day when all of my family was out of town or busy, I was feeling rather depressed. A friend recognized this and invited me to have dinner with her family. We had been friends of the family for several years and often had dinner together, but this developed into a very special meal. When I arrived I discovered the table set in the usual way for an informal dinner. But at my place I found a special plate that had printed on it "You're special." I learned that this plate was usually reserved for such commemorative occasions as birthdays, but it was put out for me on that particular day. This simple gesture of love was one of the most uplifting things they could have done. There were no elaborate words, just the symbol of their love that I knew surrounded me. My friend was able to sense that this was a time when I needed care in a personal way. We can never sense the times that people need this personal care unless we get to know the people in a very special way.

A Welcoming Church

The first perception that a newcomer has of our church is based on how it appears from the street. It is easy to become so engrossed with what goes on inside our churches that we don't recognize the positive or negative signals given by the exteriors of our buildings. Recently I consciously took note of church buildings as I traveled around several cities. Here are some questions that came from those observations.

From the Street

• From the outside, can I tell who worships here and the style of worship?

• Are there doors open to the street, or does the building give the appearance of a foreboding fortress?

• Are the doors themselves inviting, or are they dark and drab and cause me to wonder what happens behind them?

• Is it obvious where I am to go if I come to worship here for the first time?

• Is there easy access to the parking lot and ample marked parking for first-time visitors near the sanctuary entrance?

• Are there any windows, or do I feel that I will be trapped if I go inside?

• During the traditional church seasons (Christmas, Easter, etc.) is there any indication from the exterior that this church celebrates these occasions?

- Does the upkeep and maintenance of the buildings and grounds show that the members take pride in their buildings?

Real estate agents call such signals from buildings "curb appeal." When selling a home, the agents will encourage a seller to take certain measures to make sure that the home is inviting enough when viewed from the street to make the potential buyer want to see the inside. The same is true with our churches. We are not extending hospitality if we do not make our buildings inviting from the curb. We can be loving and caring to others inside our buildings, but unless we make the outsides inviting no one will come in to discover our warmth.

On the other hand, we can have great curb appeal and turn a cold shoulder to persons once they enter our doors. Consider this scenario.

We arrived at the church, and much to our surprise we found a large parking lot. We made our way to what appeared to be the education building. Inside there was a map on the wall with classroom locations.

We found the nursery for our baby. The room was clean, and the nursery worker took the baby and placed him in a crib. We did not have to sign the baby in, so we then took our older children to their classes. There we found the students and teachers engaged in an interesting activity. The teachers greeted us and then pointed us in the direction of the adult classes.

In our classroom we slipped into the back row and waited for the class to begin. People smiled at us as they moved from their groups of conversation to fill up the chairs. The teacher was interesting, and several of the class members spoke up with ideas on the subject we were discussing.

After class we picked up our older children and asked someone for directions to the sanctuary. An usher gave us a bulletin and we found a seat together on the side aisle.

The service was very much like those we'd attended before. The children went to the front for a special time with the pastor. According to the bulletin, our preschool daughter could have gone to a special program. Since she didn't know the leader or any of the children and we wouldn't know where to pick her up, she came back to sit with us. Our third-grade son tried to follow the order of worship in the adult bulletin but soon gave up and filled his time drawing on an offering envelope.

After the service we picked up the baby from the nursery. The nursery worker seemed anxious to leave, and so we went right to the car and left for home.

All in all it was a usual sort of church, very much like the others we'd visited in the city. Now it looked like we just had to decide which of these "ordinary" churches was the most convenient to our home and which had children from our children's school or neighborhood.

This church has some expressions of hospitality in place, but there are others that would certainly make the visiting family feel more welcome. Let's consider each paragraph in the scenario.

In the Parking Lot

The spacious parking lot was a welcoming site, but there could have been someone on the grounds to welcome new people and to give them any directions they needed. Signs to direct newcomers to the education building and the sanctuary entrance would have been beneficial. The map inside the building is a useful tool, but it helps to have persons stationed at the entrances to greet and welcome people personally. Some churches have a welcoming station where all visitors are greeted, with persons assigned to take them to the rooms and introduce them to their teachers.

In the Nursery

Lyle Schaller, one of the top authorities on church growth, believes that the condition of the nursery is one of the primary reasons that young families choose or reject a church. A clean nursery is certainly a welcoming signal. The nursery personnel need to recognize that their attitude toward the parent is as important as their care of the young child. Today's churches need to have a policy of doing background checks on all of their teachers and other volunteer personnel. This policy can be posted outside the door in a positive manner. Congregations who know each other well sometimes feel it is not necessary to have a sign-in sheet for the nursery. However, it is comforting for a parent to know that the child is well identified and that the adult in the nursery has knowledge of the parent's name and knows just where he or she may be found in an emergency. This can all be a part of the sign-in sheet, with an accompanying name tag for the child. Some churches provide beepers for parents. Knowing that they can easily be contacted gives the parents a sense of security.

In the Classrooms

Classroom doors also need to be inviting. The name and a picture of the teacher outside the door indicates stability in the classroom. Parents know that the teacher is regular and does not change each Sunday. There might also be information posted or leaflets available to explain what the class is studying. The interior of the classroom should be appropriate for the age level, with pictures at eye level and chairs of a comfortable height. Adult classrooms can acquire a neglected appearance if they aren't given regular attention. Don't let old curriculum pile up and keep any bulletin boards or posted notices current.

Name Tags

Churches that have name tags for their members tell newcomers two things: (1) We are proud to be a part of this community of faith; and (2) We want you to know who we are, and we'd like to get to know you too. They also help newcomers avoid the overwhelming experience of trying to learn everyone's name at once. Even with name tags, however, it is important for classes to introduce newcomers and formally welcome them into their midst. There is a precaution, however, to observe the fine line between being hospitable and smothering newcomers so that they feel obligated to return to that class even if another class is more appropriate for their needs.

In the Sanctuary

The transition from the classroom to the sanctuary would have gone much smoother had someone in the adult class offered to go with the new family to the sanctuary, helping them find it and get settled.

There are several ways that we can make our sanctuaries more welcoming. First, they must be accessible. This includes ramps and wide doors that are easy to open. And of course we need easily accessible restrooms. Both women's and men's restrooms need to be equipped for families to tend to the needs of their small children. A welcoming church provides large-print bulletins and hymnals for those with sight difficulties and either has hearing devices or reserves special places for those with hearing loss. Wide aisles and open spaces for wheel-chairs are also signs of a welcoming congregation.

Several years ago my daughter had moved to a new area of the city and was searching for a church home. She called me one day with news of how she had been received at the church she visited. All new guests were asked to raise their hands, and the ushers brought them a ticket. The ticket gave very brief information about the church, such as the hours of worship, telephone num-bers, and the Web site address. The ticket also said that a special gift awaited them at a particular table in the fellowship area after the service. When she arrived at the table, she was warmly greeted and given a jar of homemade jelly and additional information about the church.

A gift for newcomers in a good way to welcome with hospitality. The gift might be a loaf of bread, a plant, or, as my daughter received, a jar of jelly. Sometimes these gifts are given on site and sometimes they are de-livered to the home during the following week.

Another way of welcoming is to offer a tour of the facility after the service. The tour not only helps to ori-ent the newcomers to the buildings, but during the tour different programs, events, and ministries of the church can be casually introduced. I even chanced upon a church that was holding a garage and craft sale one Saturday. To my surprise, there were church members everywhere, not just behind the tables selling the items. Many of them simply milled with the crowd, making sure that every-one found what they were looking for. They also told them that tours of the sanctuary were being offered at any time they would like. During these tours the banners and symbols in the sanctuary were introduced. The tour also gave people who were not familiar with the church a chance to have a look-see in a nonthreatening atmosphere.

If a church hopes to reach out to young families, then the members and staff must have a positive attitude toward them in worship and there must be accommodations to make it easy for the children to be a part of worship. Here are some suggestions:

- Encourage families to sit close to the front so that the children can see what's happening.

- Provide booster seats for families to take to their pew, allowing children to sit higher and see over the back's of pews.

- Include children of all ages as ushers and greeters. They can act as apprentices while they are young, standing and serving alongside an adult or with their family.

- Provide rockers at the back or sides of the sanctuary so that a parent can soothe a restless child.

- Provide packets with crayons and such for young children.

- Provide pads and pencils in the pews for adults and children to take sermon notes.

- If children go to another room for part of the service, include the location in the bulletin so that parents feel comfortable about finding their children after the service.

- Develop a young reader's bulletin, following the design of the adult bulletin but including more detail's of what happens during the service. Also provide blank spaces with suggestions for notes that they might take at various times during the service.

Informational Materials

Churches produce a mammoth amount of informational materials. These have become more important as our churches move from intimate, community congregations to large churches drawing complete strangers from many areas, of a city. As we move into the new millennium we must look at updated methods of disbursing our information. This will include e-mail and Web sites, radio and television, as well as printed materials.

I visit numerous churches during the course of a year, and I am often with the congregations during the Sunday morning service. One of the first things I notice as I review the bulletin is the paper on which it is printed. If the paper is such that the printing shows through from the other side, I not only have difficulty reading it, but I also have the impression that there is a lack of pride in the congregation. If we feel strongly about our mission for Christ, then we will let that pride show in everything that goes out of the church office. Grammar and spelling will be correct, and materials will be clear and well organized. All information and calendars will be kept up to date, and the presentation will be eye appealing. How would Christ want his church represented in the twenty-first century? How does the informational material say "Welcome, we are proud of our church, and we would like for you to be a part of our church family"?

And Other Ways

Here are a few other points to look for when making your church more hospitable:

- Be sure that hallways and meeting rooms are bright. Sometimes we become so accustomed to dim lighting in our hallways that we don't recognize the impression that it gives to newcomers.

- Church parlors need to be nicely furnished but not so elaborate that people are afraid to use them. We must also exercise stewardship of space. Perhaps church parlors should be called gathering rooms if we truly want them to be hospitable.
- Make it clear to all newcomers that you expect persons to visit several classes before deciding which adult class they will join.
- Train volunteers to greet people and answer the phone in the office. Stress the importance of greeting in a friendly manner. They can answer any general questions and then pass other requests on to the proper person. When staff persons are stressed by answering the day-to-day details, they can lose their patience more easily.

Without unconditional welcome, we are not a true church. And unconditional welcome can only come when we truly open ourselves to Christ and all of his teachings. There are several faith statements or creeds that have come to us over the years. The beginning of "A Modern Affirmation" states:

> *Where the Spirit of the Lord is,*
> *There is the one true church, apostolic and*
> *universal...*

CHAPTER 4

Hospitality of Speaking and Listening

Let my words and my thoughts be pleasing to you, Lord,
because you are my mighty rock and my protector.

Psalm 19:14 (CEV)

We usually think of communication as the words that come out of our mouths. In fact, all too often we don't even listen to what another person is saying because we are so busy trying to formulate the words for our own reply. In reality, communication is 7 percent verbal content, 38 percent tone of voice, and 55 percent body language. In order to understand another person, we must take all of these into account. We must also recognize this when we try to convey a message.

Do we listen with the intent to understand, or the intent to reply? Communication must be within the frame of reference of the other person. One way to ensure hospitality in communication is to agree that you will always restate the other person's point to that person's satisfaction before stating your own point. Most disagreements are actually misunderstandings.

Somewhere I heard a definition of hospitality that went something like this: *Hospitality is showing how much you care for another person before expounding on how much you know.* An example of this is found in John 13:1–20, when Jesus washed the disciples' feet. Jesus could have sent out for someone to wash their feet and spent that time expounding on the importance of loving one another. Instead, he simply bound the towel around his waist, picked up the basin, and went about demonstrating his love and concern. Has our concept of Christianity become so cerebral that we ignore the experiential? It was through the experiential ministry of Christ that the word actually shone through. The prophets had spoken, and the law had been written, but it took the Immanuel, in human form, to bring us the true experience of God. Unless we continue to pass on that understanding of God, we may as well be functioning in the pre-Christ concepts of our religion.

Using Words

Words can hurt and words can heal. Too often we fail to recognize how words affect other people. We have become so comfortable with our own expressions that we only hear them with our own ears—ears that have been conditioned by years of custom and tradition. What do our words say about hospitality?

We need to realize that the Bible came to its present form through oral tradition first and then in written word, but at all times reflecting the experiences and culture of each generation of storytellers. The images and stories of the Bible recall the patriarchal culture and society of that day.

In reality the Bible contains a variety of images for God, many of which we seldom use. I have seen a list of more than two hundred images. Here is a sampling: Creator, Preserver, Light, Fortress, Refuge, Word, Wisdom, Redeemer, Protector, Shepherd, Mother Hen, Guardian, Guide, Healer, Comforter, and Provider. All of these images reflect hospitality.

The church is gradually recognizing that we must make changes in our language in order to help folks hear the message. Often our language limits us in unconscious ways. We fail to recognize the power that words have over us. These power words may be used to dominate others. When the words "sound right" to us, we assume that they are the right words to use, because we want things to be the way that sounds right to us.

Sadly, the English language does not have a nongender pronoun. There are three ways that we can deal with pronouns for God. We can (1) use male or female pronouns exclusively, (2) alternate male and female pronouns (which can cloud the clarity as to whom the pronoun refers), and (3) avoid the pronouns for God completely by using God's name or restructuring the sentence.

When preparing the manuscript for my first book, my editor suggested that I go back and eliminate all gender references to God by either using the name God again or restructuring the sentence. My first reaction was "Why should I? I recognize the pronouns as terms for a nongender deity." The words sounded right to me. I suspect that my resistance also involved a bit of possessiveness over my manuscript. After all, I had birthed the manuscript, and who was the editor to ask me to change it so drastically? I had lots to learn!

When I came down off my high horse, I began to view the manuscript from a reader's perspective. I decided that, even though the masculine pronouns for God did not bother me and probably did not bother most of the public, if there was one person out there who might pick up the book and decide not to read it because of the masculine pronouns, then it was worth going through and changing them. Interestingly enough, when I later pointed this out to persons who had read the book, they expressed surprised that I had gone through and made such changes. They did not recognize the absence of those pronouns.

Now, sixteen years later, I find myself uncomfortable when I hear a gender pronoun used in place of the name of God. I've even taken little surveys and counted the number of times that the word *he* was used to refer to God in a scripture passage or hymn. Then I wonder why we feel comfortable using any pronoun for God so many times when we could use God's name instead. Are we fearful of repeating God's name? Some people tell me that it's monotonous to hear God's name used over and over. It seems to me that it is just as monotonous to hear the pronoun used over and over. And doesn't the use of God's name make a better witness to our religious faith than a pronoun, no matter what the gender?

About two years ago I began singing the doxology by substituting the word *God* in each place that the masculine pronoun is normally sung. This has caused no problems in my highly traditional church. In fact, I'm not even sure that those sitting around me recognize the difference. However, it has opened a whole new concept of God to me, because it awakens my awareness of God each time I repeat God's name.

We don't recognize that the loss of familiar terms and phrases actually brings about a sort of grieving process. In reality we need to exercise hospitality and allow the word changes to happen slowly, enabling the grieving to take place. The gradual change also allows us to become comfortable with the new terms.

Some years ago we seldom used the words *spouse* or *sibling.* These terms were used in the academic world, or we found them on forms that we filled out for the government. Now we feel more comfortable referring to our *spouse* or our *sibling.* We are becoming accustomed to hearing the terms, and consequently we begin to use them ourselves.

I recall a family where an adult child decided that she wanted to change her given name. She filled out the legal application and asked her family to call her by her new name. There was a good bit of resistance at first, and there were many times that the family slipped and used her original name. But as the years progressed they became comfortable with the new name, and now her new name seems to suit her personality.

Similarly, in the church we have periodically gone through a grieving process with language. We spent nearly three hundred fifty years using primarily the King James Version of the Bible. During that time the transition of religious language from one generation to the next came fairly easily, but when the Revised Standard Version was completed in 1952, it took several years before it had wide acceptance. Today we have several translations coming out at one time, and we are beginning to appreciate each of them for their own value. But it took years of grieving over the comfort zone that certain words held for us, and we still fall back on some of our Elizabethan language, particularly for the scripture that we learned as children. There is nothing wrong with this as long as we realize that we are using it because it is a comfortable language for us and not because it is the only viable translation. We must realize that some-one new to the faith is not likely to find this translation comforting.

Now we are going through the same sort of griev-ing process over much of our liturgical language. The Roman Catholic Church made a move to change their liturgy from Latin to English some years ago. This met with complaints from many persons who found the Latin language very comfortable, even though they were not proficient in Latin.

The language of our liturgy and hymns not only uses pronouns and images that reflect the experiences and cultures of those in the past, but it also often gives the impression of a closed group of people. Dr. Leonard Sweet, dean of Drew Theological School, suggests that we might rephrase Fanny Crosby's song "Blessed Assur-ance." Instead of using the show-and-tell evangelistic words "This is my story," he suggests that we use more inviting and inclusive words, words that help people see how God is already at work in their lives. He sugges-tions the words, "You are God's story; you are God's song."[1]

As our Protestant liturgical language is giving way to a more common form, we feel that something is taken away from our faith, and so we grieve. Allowing that process to happen is a very hospitable act.

Language is actually a vehicle by which God enters our human experience and relationships. For some people the traditional language carries out this mission, but for many newcomers to the church, we must change the language so that the same message comes across in a way that allows them to grasp it.

Body Language and Vocal Tone

Sometimes we say words that are expected, but our tone of voice can actually carry a different meaning. A different tone of voice can turn a complimentary phrase into a sarcastic remark or put-down in the ear of the listener.

In chapter 8 of the gospel of Mark, Jesus becomes exasperated with the lack of understanding on the part of the Pharisees and then asks the disciples if they understand what he's talking about. The remarks by Jesus can be read in a tone of voice that indicates weariness in having to explain, or they can be read with a tone of pity or even of anger. They can also be read as expressing sadness and concern that the message is not being understood, particularly at a time when he recognized his impending death.

Our tone of voice in teaching, in liturgical reading, and in reading of the scripture can also send a message that such experiences are humdrum, with no real value to the reader. This is why it is important to have some sort of training for laypersons who lead in a worship service and for teachers who read scripture in the classroom.

Vocal language is not the only way that we offer hospitality. Jesus himself recognized the importance of body language and of our acts and deeds. He reprimanded the Pharisees for this many times, calling them hypocrites because their actions seemed pious yet their intent was devious.

Attention to our body language is important, whether we are talking one-on-one with a person or speaking before a large group. Eye contact is one of the first signals of lack of interest. When we never look a person in the eye we can create an inhospitable atmosphere.

With our busy schedules and complex lives, we overload our brain circuits. As we recognize the overload, we often try to save time by solving some other problem while listening to someone. This usually translates into some form of body language. It also catches us unaware when we need to respond to the person, having no clue as to what has been said. Conscious eye contact helps to keep you on key and alert to the conversation. You may also find it helpful to mentally catalog just what is being said, trying to grasp the actual message that the speaker is sending and not just the words. Paying attention to the other person's body language will help you be a more attentive listener.

It's easy to ignore your body language when speaking before a group of people. You may be so nervous that you can't think of much more than the words you have to speak. Or you may subconsciously think that you have everyone's attention anyway and not recognize the importance of body language. This can often happen with a memorized speech, if you allow it to become rote or if you have to concentrate hard in order to draw the words from your memory bank. The more relaxed you are, the more comfortable your audience will be. You will need to develop a style of delivery that suits you best so that you create a hospitable atmosphere.

All of my life I've had difficulty with memorization. Consequently I've learned that I create a more hospitable atmosphere if I either speak from notes, forming my sentences as I go along, or read a speech. I have found, however, that hand-held note cards are much less formidable than a stack of papers when speaking to a group. I put my notes on 4 x 6" cards, which are easy to hold in my hand. I use a different card for each thought or for a group of thoughts. The cards become a sort of outline for me. I may decide during the course of a lesson or workshop to rearrange the outline, perhaps because of a particular response from the group or because of a time restraint. It is easy to shuffle the cards right on the spot and draw up something that I'd planned to use later in the event. Or I may realize that a subject has been covered during a discussion or question period. Then I simply skip over those cards as I come to them. This method particularly has helped me when, during a longer event and after the first meeting with a group, I realized that I should approach the subject from a different direction. Had my notes been printed on sheets of paper, I would have had to retype them or draw confusing arrows back and forth between topics. Even when I know my subject well, I rely on my cards from time to time, making sure that I have covered every aspect of the theme.

I recognize that my style of delivery is more informal than that of some speakers, but the response that I receive indicates that the way I tailor the contents of my presentation to the particular needs of the participants is more appreciated than a "canned speech." This creates a space where people are welcomed and feel cared for. The workshop atmosphere becomes hospitable because it is tailored to their needs.

You might consider some other body language suggestions for creating a hospitable atmosphere when you speak before a group. Wear clothing similar to those to whom you are speaking. They will feel more comfortable if you conform in some way, and clothing is a simple way to do this. In effect, you are saying, "I affirm you," and they will therefore be more inclined to listen to you.

Your respect for the time schedule is another way to create a hospitable climate. Remember that they have other obligations that you should honor. However, you don't want to rush through your presentation and give a feeling that your time would be better spent elsewhere. One example of body language that signals rushing is obviously looking at your watch. In order to keep track of the time without being conspicuous, I always wear a watch with a large face, and I usually turn my watch to the underside of my arm. This allows me to check the time without obviously turning my arm over.

There are several body positions that create a negative atmosphere, signaling a closed attitude. All my life I've been conscious of my long arms, and I constantly have to fight myself to keep from standing with them crossed. I recognize that such body language is actually self-consciousness on my part, but those listening to me do not know this, and they are likely to feel that I'm not open to hearing their opinions if I stand with my arms crossed.

The manner in which we sit also signals our interest. When you lean forward you indicate an interest in what is being said, but when you obviously draw back or even lean back in a chair, you remove yourself from what's happening and thereby send a negative signal. Pacing also creates an uneasy atmosphere. It unsettles the other person, creating a sense of desire for escape.

When trying to develop hospitable space for others, perhaps we should consider what someone has said: "I cannot hear what you are saying because your actions speak so loudly they drown out your words."

Listening

Whether a brief one-on-one encounter or within a large group, a conversation must be a two-way street. This reality is often overlooked in churches. We are so convinced that our opinion on a subject is the only viable one that we spend all of our time and effort trying to persuade the other person instead of listening. Unless we are open to hearing all opinions, we neglect hospitality.

In order to foster the development of faith, we must create a listening atmosphere. An important aspect of our faith growth is inquiry. Without an inquiring mind, faith becomes stale. Normally we move into this period of spiritual searching during our late teens and early twenties. Many churches squelch any open questioning of beliefs. Consequently, we lose young adults during this time because the church does not listen openly to their inquiry.

We must recognize that some people think as they speak and some must think before they speak. Those of us who think as we speak often feel uncomfortable when there is a lull in the conversation. However, when we do not allow time for persons to think through what they want to say, we may appear to have little interest in their opinions. These lulls are actually good readiness for the listening that is essential to hospitality. Whether in the church, in the home, or anywhere else in our daily lives, we sometimes have the mistaken idea that hospitality involves being sure that conversation flows constantly, when in fact a constant chatter can wear a person out. There are times when the interchange of ideas keeps a conversation flowing at a steady pace. *Interchange* is the key word here. Lulls in conversation are better than simply filling up space with chatter.

The lack of an open, listening ear creates an inhospitable atmosphere. I recall a conversation with a woman who said that she did not want to take another class with a particular teacher. I wondered why, because I had heard reports that this person was a good teacher. The woman had taken an extensive study that surveyed the complete Bible over several months under this teacher, and she said that she got very little from the study. During one of the early sessions there was a discussion on the first chapters of Genesis. The leader of the study cut her short as she was sharing her thoughts about creation. The leader said, "That is not the right understanding of creation. You simply cannot believe that and be a Christian." The woman said that she no longer cared whether the teacher was right or wrong. When she was not allowed to express her thoughts, she no longer gave any credibility to the leader's comments. Reflecting on her conversation, I realized that the other people who had affirmed this teacher were either not of an inquiring mind or held the same theological views as the teacher.

There are several attitudes that actually block communication:

- Demanding a certain belief or attitude.
- Using sarcasm.
- Giving advice without being asked.
- Offering advice as THE solution rather than as a suggestion to be considered.
- Smoothing over problems with distractions or platitudes.
- Using a know-it-all attitude.
- Concentrating on something else.
- Suddenly changing the subject.

Some years ago someone coined the phrase *active listening*. This type of listening involves your attitude as well as your attention. As an active listener you are not just absorbing information. Instead, you are listening in such a manner as to encourage the speaker to continue expressing his or her thoughts. In order to do this you must:

Minimize speaking

Maximize attention

Mention what you hear being said

It takes a big dose of active listening to create a hospitable atmosphere in meetings. Meetings in churches can be even more inhospitable than in business situations. Perhaps this is partly because we expect a church meeting to be different. After all, Christ modeled hospitality. But church meetings are not different without some conscious effort to make them so. Here are some suggestions:

- Distribute a printed agenda before the meeting. This helps persons formulate thoughts and dampens the explosive atmosphere that surprises bring about.

- Repeat what has been said in a summarized form so that everyone is clear about what has transpired.

- Learn to use discernment instead of parliamentary procedure. When we take a vote, we immediately set up opposing sides, whereas discernment helps us to discover God's will as a community. The book *Discerning God's Will Together* by Danny Morris and Charles Olsen suggests these steps in discernment:

   (1) Framing—What exactly are you trying to discern?

   (2) Grounding—What value determines that this decision be made?

   (3) Shedding—What preconceived notions, biases, and predetermined conclusions must I set aside to be truly open to God's will in this case?

   (4) Rooting—What Christian tradition and/or biblical stories speak to this situation?

   (5) Listening—What do others say/feel about the situation? Listen to all sides of the questions and find out about the needs.

(6) Exploring—Creatively explore all possibilities.

(7) Improving—Looking at each option and, with prayer, improve on it until it is the very best.

(8) Weighing—Sort out and test the options or paths in response to the leading of God's spirit.

(9) Closing—Closing the exploration and identifying possible selection.

(10) Resting—Laying choice before the heart of God and determining whether it brings a sense of peace and movement toward God or distress and movement away from God.[2]

• From time to time interject a statement that connects what is taking place in the meeting with the mission statement of the church. This may be a statement such as, "This project helps us fulfill our mission statement by caring for God's people." Or you may have copies of the mission statement and ask the group to read it and find how the project fulfills the mission.

• Format the agenda to include spiritual enrichment. Charles Olsen, in his book *Transforming Church Boards into Communities of Spiritual Leaders,* suggests that church meetings need to be different. He offers several models, one patterned after a worship service. This format would open the meeting with praise expressed in song or through a psalm or litany. Then there would be opportunity for story, either a scripture study that is appropriate for the setting of the meeting or perhaps sharing various ways that God has been evident in the life of the church or in individual lives since the group last met. The actual "business agenda" would become the offering, that which you offer up to God. And a summary of decisions that have been made may be considered the "sending forth" or benediction. This puts the business of what would be a boring or explosive meeting into a spiritual atmosphere. It is surprising how one comes away from such a meeting refreshed and challenged to carry out the ministry of Christ.

Before we leave the hospitality of listening, I must call attention to the opportunity for creating this atmosphere in our church services. We must be intentional about designing worship to allow listening, the listening that is most important, listening to God. Churches do this in different ways. If your church observes the Lord's supper every time you meet, then you most likely have a quiet listening time in place. Some churches design a separate, early-morning communion service that is primarily meditative. Other churches establish a meditation time before or at the beginning of the service. Your church may have a tradition of visiting among yourselves as you enter the sanctuary, but quiet moments may be written into the service after the call to worship, setting such listening time aside. Contemporary services tend to be celebrative. However, it is important to work some period of private listening into this form of worship also. This may be done during a pastoral prayer or after the delivery of the message.

It does take a concentrated effort to make sure that your church offers a listening atmosphere, for without it we cannot be a hospitable church.

CHAPTER 5

Hospitality of Serving

So Jesus told them, "Foreign kings order their people around, and powerful rulers call themselves everyone's friends. But don't be like them. The most important one of you should be like the least important, and your leader should be like a servant."

Luke 22:25–26 (CEV)

The hospitality of serving borders on spiritual leadership. The story of Esther in the Bible has more to tell us about hospitality than we often recognize. Esther was the wife of the Persian King Xerxes (or Ahasuerus). Her cousin Mordecai, who was a palace official, had raised her. According to his instructions, Esther did not let it be known that she was Jewish. The highest official of the king's court, Haman, tricked the king into giving permission for all Jews to be killed. Mordecai sent a message informing Esther of what was about to happen to the Jews. He told her that perhaps she was queen for just such an occasion. Esther risked her life to intervene, and the Jews were saved.

Esther served her people and, in so doing, created an open and caring surrounding for her people. She used the opportunity that was at hand. Hospitality does not come from a set of rules or from a book, but it comes from the heart. With hospitality we must let the heart lead in service.

Serving needs to be a conscious act, one that is done with intention. Our purpose in serving must go even beyond the desire to be hospitable to others. We must serve as an act of worship. A scripture that is popular as a greeting posted in the home comes from Joshua 24:15b. In the New Revised Standard Version it is translated "...as for me and my household, we will serve the LORD." The Contemporary English Version, however, translates it, "My family and I are going to worship and obey the LORD!" What better way to translate serving than as a worshipful act! Serving should not be a matter of obligation, but rather a desire to express our worship and love for God through action. Jesus expressed it well when he said, "Whenever you did it for any of my people, no matter how unimportant they seemed, you did it for me." (Matthew 25:40, CEV).

Gifts for Serving

In the church, we serve in different ways. If we are to take Christ's challenge seriously, we will put service at the heart of our ministry. We will recognize that we are on this earth for just such a purpose as this, to serve. It is through service that we reach out to others. But we cannot have true from-the-heart service without recognizing our own gifts that can be used for God. They go hand in hand. Knowing our gifts and recognizing our opportunities for service are the head and heart of our ministry. Putting this into action is the hands and feet of our ministry.

In every church there are persons with varying gifts from God. As Paul said in Romans 12:6, "We have gifts that differ according to the grace given to us" (NRSV). A part of our challenge as a church is to help persons discover their gifts and challenge them to put those gifts into action. There are several programs available for seminars or class studies on discovering your gifts. The one that I find helpful yet simple to use is Patricia Brown's workbook *Spirit Gifts* (Abingdon Press, 1996). It has a leader's guide that helps you use the workbook with a group. Some churches use programs similar to this as part of their membership course. When people recognize the varying opportunities to be a meaningful part of the church, then they see themselves as welcomed. But they do want to be able to make that choice themselves.

In the past, different aspects of ministry were planned by a governing body of the church and then persons were sought out to fill those opportunities for service. This often required a begging attitude in order to get people to take leadership responsibilities in those areas. In the new world of volunteers, churches are developing their ministries in a manner that allows persons to serve in areas where they feel called and where they have a passion. In these churches, when someone comes forward with a passion for some ministry, a conference is set to discuss the proposed ministry. Once it is determined that the proposed ministry is in line with the church's mission, the person is given the go-ahead. Help is provided in the form of resources and any training that may be needed. Such an approach requires the

governing body and staff leadership to constantly review the church's mission. The person who heads the
ministry is brought back for review periodically, for affirmation and to monitor the progress. The plus of such
a plan is the dedication of the person to the cause or
project. When there is a passion for ministry, we usually
find the Holy Spirit at work!

We sometimes think that we cannot serve others
unless we are perfect ourselves. This seems particularly
true in the church. As a staff member in Christian
education, I received many negative responses to my
request for Sunday school teachers. One of the most
common was, "I don't know enough about the Bible
myself!" We think we are inadequate for the job.

Yet God has shown us differently in the past. We
can offer our services to others without being fully whole
ourselves. Let's look at persons in our biblical heritage
who might have said that they could not serve because
they were not "good enough." Abraham and Sarah certainly felt that they could not become the parents of a
great nation when they were not even able to produce
one offspring, but God proved otherwise. If someone
had told the slave Joseph that he would someday be
responsible for all of Egypt's wealth, he would probably
have laughed. Moses so much as told God that he was
not the one to represent the people before Pharaoh because he had a speech difficulty. Rahab's previous ca-
reer of prostitution would not seem to qualify her to be
an ancestor of King David. Esther did not feel capable
of convincing the king to save the Hebrews until she
was reminded that she might be in that place for just
such a time. Jonah did not think he was the one to de-
liver God's message to the people of Nineveh, but God
used a big fish to convince him. When God called him,
Jeremiah complained that he was only a child. Mary was
probably overwhelmed with the responsibility of her

impending delivery. Peter's denial made his leadership potential improbable, but Jesus chose him as the foundation of the church. When God calls, we will be much happier when we answer that call.

Once people make a commitment to serve, we as leaders in the church sometimes tend to forget about them. We are so relieved to have persons to "fill the slots" that we send them out to the field to toil, perhaps with a few tools, but then we turn to others who are struggling to find a ministry of service. In reality we must keep in constant contact with those who serve. Once they are on the job, they really need the support.

I recall a teacher who worked with me in a midweek children's program. Somewhere around the middle of the year I discovered that she was not aware of our supply room and had been buying all of her supplies out of her own pocket. We had given a tour of the supply room in the fall during a training event for all of the teachers, but she had not been able to attend. I had also given her a handbook that had information about the supply room, but she had not had time to read the book. One might argue that reading the handbook was her own responsibility, especially since she had missed the meeting. Yet my role in hospitality to those who serve under my leadership should have included close enough contact with her to allow me to realize her ignorance. I should have given her more assistance earlier in the year. Hospitality to leaders is essential in a church. We need not only to give them support in their work, but also support and love when they are having personal problems. We must be aware of their time schedules, working to help them serve even with the time restraints that today's commitments require. We must look at serving from the volunteer's point of view and affirm them as they carry out their ministry. There are various ways to do this:

- Provide refreshments at appropriate times.
- Celebrate their birthdays and other special occasions in their lives.
- Make them aware of our prayers.
- Recognize their ministry before the congregation.
- Publicize the "fruits" of their ministry.
- Provide child care when necessary.
- Provide resources and supplies for their ministry.

Remember that Jesus saw to the needs of his disciples. In John 13:1–17 we read the story of how Jesus washed feet that were tired and dirty from the roads they had walked. What greater leader of leaders can we learn from than him? We must offer hospitality to our leaders. By so doing we help the individual, and we also lift up serving as an affirmative way to express faith.

Whole Church Passion

It is essential that we create a passion for the hospitality of serving throughout the whole church family. I know of one church that had grown from a small, one-room country church to a congregation of about seven hundred members. They had built a larger sanctuary and outgrown it, and now they were ready to enlarge their facility again. The wise leadership of the church encouraged the congregation to plan to build a sanctuary for a mission congregation as they prepared for building their own sanctuary. This hand-in-hand ministry strengthened the congregation. They not only extended hospitality to another congregation, but as guests visited their church they recognized a family of believers that was open to all of God's people.

When we get hung up in reporting, all we can see is the amount of money we have raised or how persons have served in "approved" mission opportunities. If we are to challenge our people to live out their Christian calling in all aspects of life, then we should recognize their service in other ministries in the community besides those within the confines of the church. It amazed one congregation when they conducted a survey to discover just where their people were involved in ministry. Besides the ministry that the church itself sponsored, there were more than thirty other ministries in which their members participated.

When we reach beyond our local church boundaries in ministry it changes us. We naturally become more open to others, and this then changes our manner of hospitality. Serving others makes a profound difference in lives. If we are to affect the lives of those in our churches, challenging them to follow Christ's commands, then we must be about creating opportunities for service. We must also be about helping them to know that we appreciate their ministry and giving them assistance as they learn how to carry out that ministry. When we do not do this, we create an inhospitable atmosphere.

There are a couple of precautions about emphasizing specific mission opportunities. It is easy for leadership to develop such a strong conviction for a specific mission that they become blind to all others. We can also become so intent on serving that we overlook all other aspects of the church, simply carrying out the obligation that we sense to be our duty as Christians. In either case, we create an inhospitable atmosphere. We create animosity and an unbalanced ministry.

Spreading the Table

It was a lovely day outside when parents and children gathered to enjoy an afternoon of learning. As we walked through the doors, no one greeted us, but we did find a choice of sandwich makings that would appeal to both children and adults laid out on a table. We made our own sandwiches and moved into the fellowship hall. The room was dimly lit, and there were several tables set up at one end of the room. Folding chairs surrounded the long, narrow tables, and a side table was set up with cups, ice, and sodas. Families were settling in for a meal before the learning event.

On another day I encountered an entirely different church setting. The same sort of family learning event was planned, but even from a distance we knew that something exciting was happening in the church. As we approached the brightly lit fellowship hall, we heard inviting music and saw festive tables. Someone greeted us at the door and asked us to make a name tag. Then we were invited to pick up a plate with a sandwich and sit at a table of our choosing. Fruit and drinks were already on the tables, and there were festive napkins and a decoration in the center of each table that combined small toys with garden flowers. Long tables had been pushed together, side by side, to create square tables that promoted conversation. On the table were some printed suggestions for dialogue that would help us become better acquainted with our fellow diners. When everyone had gathered, we sang a blessing together and began our meal with our new friends.

Ingredients as simple as sandwiches and fruit in two different settings became two different meals. Spreading the table in a hospitable way involves more than simply setting up tables and chairs and putting out the food.

Another church introduced midweek dinners with classes and children's events before and after the meal. The purpose for the meal was fellowship. However, there was no direction or suggestion for making the meal more than a quick-food service in a noncommercial setting. Finally, after several months of good eats but little fellowship, someone took it upon himself to initiate a common prayer and to take time to find out about any birthdays or anniversaries being celebrated that week. Although this was a minor addition to the mealtime, a surprising number of people expressed appreciation for the hospitality. They said that the addition created a friendlier atmosphere and made it easier to talk with people they did not know.

When feeding folks in the church, creating an atmosphere of caring and welcome is as important as combining the ingredients. This usually doesn't just happen any more than food just happens to cook itself. In order to reflect this, some churches have even changed the title of the person who coordinates and/or prepares the meals. Instead of food service director or dietitian, churches are adopting such titles as director of hospitality or church hostess/host. Where budget permits, churches make this a paid staff position, expanding it to include a watchful eye to determine hospitality in all areas of the church. Such a move recognizes the importance of serving the whole person, not just the physical body.

Persons with leadership responsibilities in food preparation in the church need to recognize that they are offering a true ministry, not only to those who eat the food, but also to those with whom they work in preparing the food. My husband has worked in this area in four different churches, usually in a volunteer leadership position. He works best when he has several people who help him on a regular basis instead of a different pick-up crew for each meal. A community develops among the regular helpers, and we soon find ourselves involved in loving and caring for each other. There is an atmosphere of laughter and fun and fellowship over potato peeling and tea preparation, but there is also an underlying sense of the Spirit that develops as the relationships mature into a small-group fellowship. When one is in the hospital, the word spreads and we are all in prayer. When a parent experiences frustration over a child's behavior, we lend a listening ear and step in to help where we can. There are joys to celebrate and heartaches to share. And when the season of regular dinners comes to an end, we usually have a big festive occasion—to do what? To eat and fellowship!

Sharing the Joy of Serving

As a child my mother passed on to me an admonition that her father had given her. I've used it often and only found one other person who had received the same instruction. She would tell me, "Make yourself useful as well as ornamental." And I would immediately remember to ask my hostess if there was something that I could do to help. Early on I learned the joy of serving no matter where I am, and to this day I seek out opportunities to serve when I go to someone else's home. Serving changes its complexion. Through serving with others I have enjoyed many delightful conversations that could never have come about had I remained in the position of a privileged guest!

Sometimes we are most hospitable when we allow others to serve. It can change the whole perspective of service, as shown in the following story that was shared by Julia Kuhn Wallace in the devotional magazine *Alive Now*.

Led by a Child

A congregation I served in Virginia participated in a program named CARITAS (Congregations Around Richmond Involved to Assure Shelter). For a given week during the winter months, we offered our church as a shelter for the homeless. It was quite a commitment, because the congregation provided the dinner every evening, set up cots for the people to sleep on at night, and served breakfast every morning.

By the third year of the program, it was hard to recruit hosts. For the third week in a row, the coordinator asked for a member of the congregation to host on Tuesday evening. Finally, a little hand went up. It happened to be my seven-year-old daughter, Amanda. I remember her saying, "I'll do it. I'll be glad to do that." There was a moment of silence. Then the coordinator said, "I know you'll be a great host, Amanda. You'll have all the help you'll need. I'm sure of it." Indeed, she did get the help she needed. Amanda's sign-up list filled up first. The night that she was to host we got there early and set the tables. As she made sure that the napkins were folded just right and that everything looked perfect, she explained, "This is for our guests, you know." After we had finished our preparations and were waiting for the guests to arrive, I saw Amanda walk around the cots, straightening the beds and plumping the pillows.

When the guests arrived, she was waiting at the door. Amanda shook her guests' hands, introduced herself, told them how glad she was they had come, and asked them their names. When mealtime came, Amanda invited everyone to stand in a circle and hold hands and then asked for someone to bless the food. One of the guests said, "I will." After the prayer, Amanda asked, "Who would like to help serve the food?" The church volunteers had always passed the food through a serving window in the kitchen. Involving the guests in serving really changed how all of us—volunteers and guests—thought about this ministry. Rather than being something we did for our guests or to them, CARITAS became something we did with them. In that moment I realized that though we were participating in the program to get close and personal with our guests, we had been afraid of it.

Amanda helped church members see that we were offering more than just shelter. We were offering a place of warmth and relationship. Amanda had listened to what we had been saying in church about Jesus loving, touching, healing, and feeding people and the fact that we are called to be in ministry with the people around us. She took it quite literally. We knew it in our heads. She knew it in her heart. Her actions of calling people by name, introducing herself, making connections with people, and involving them made real what church is about. She led us into an understanding of the real reason we were there. She opened our eyes.[3]

The elaborateness of the chance to serve, on our part and on the part of our guests, is not so important as simply providing that opportunity. Jesus pointed that out when he brought the disciples' attention to the contrast of gifts being placed in the treasury at the temple. He said that the widow who gave less than a penny had given more than all of the rich people. The value of the gift is in the giving. The value of service is in the serving (Mark 12:41–44; Luke 21:1–4).

CHAPTER 6

Hospitality of Comforting and Healing

"...to tell the good news to the poor...to announce freedom for prisoners, to give sight to the blind, to free everyone who suffers..."

Luke 4:18 (CEV)

A preteen attending vacation Bible school became exasperated and said to some adults in the kitchen, "This is what I think of Bible school." With that she crumpled a paper cup and threw it on the floor. One of the adults simply picked up the cup, smoothed it out, and put it in his hand. Offering it back to the girl he said, "And this is what we think of you."[4] What a gift of hospitality and healing for the girl's troubled soul. Had Jesus been working at that vacation Bible school, he probably would have acted in much the same manner as that adult.

In the fourth chapter of John we find the story of a time when Jesus sat beside a well and had a conversation with a woman at the noon hour. Jesus asked the woman for water, an unusual thing in that situation. In the first place, a Jewish man did not speak to unknown women in public. This woman also came at noontime, which was not the usual time for women to draw water from the well. The woman probably postponed her trips in order to avoid the knowing eyes and wagging tongues of other women, for her lifestyle was not respected. Jesus was also in Samaria, a country much hated by the Jewish community, and so conversation with any Samaritan would have been frowned upon by other Jews. But Jesus did speak to the woman, not only asking her for water, but also offering healing for her soul. Jesus offered an opportunity for the woman to hold her head up proudly and once again become a part of the community.

There are times in each of our lives when we need encouragement or comforting. It is very important to be alert to the needs of those around us. We never know when God may be calling us to be angels unaware.

Encouragement

David, during his service time to King Saul, had many problems. The king was very jealous of him and several times tried to kill him. The king's son, Jonathan, had been a good friend of David's for many years. Throughout all of the conflicts that David had with the king, Jonathan continued to love David and to encourage him, even amidst the attempted murders. Jonathan knew that David had the potential to make a good king, and time and again he encouraged him (1 Samuel 18–23).

Encouragement in the face of crisis is a crucial element in hospitality. This is particularly true today when extended families live at such distances. The age-old support systems have been broken, and many families have no one to fulfill this role. This is the case with young families that are required to move in order to establish their careers. It is also true for aging persons, when the family has moved elsewhere or they have moved away from the family in an attempt to find more economical living on a fixed income. The hospitable church does not wait for these people to come to them in crisis, but is open and searching for opportunities to lay the foundation even before the crisis. It also takes preventative measures to combat crisis. Here are some ideas that some churches have found useful:

- Sponsor support groups such as divorce recovery, alcohol and drug abuse, parents of mentally challenged persons, caregivers of persons with chronic or fatal illnesses, survivors of abuse, parents of children with learning disabilities, persons with job loss, and such.
- Maintain a loan closet. There is a lot of furniture and equipment that is necessary in short-term situations, such as visiting grandchildren and homebound care. These can be shared among the church family.
- Provide van or bus transportation for those who cannot drive themselves.
- Install electronic hearing devices for the hearing challenged and/or provide sign language interpreter.
- Install ramps and elevators for those who are physically challenged.
- Offer telephone Sunday school class for the homebound. The church can arrange for regular conference calls to be set up weekly by a telephone company. These not only allow persons to continue their learning, but also act as a smaller community for those

who are homebound. Often a caregiver in the home takes part in the class through a speakerphone.

- Provide day care for adults as well as for children, or classes/assistance in identifying and finding good day care.
- Plan common meals during holidays. Such joyful occasions can be the loneliest times of the year for persons without family or with a recent loss.
- Offer baby-sitting courses that teach the emotional and spiritual care of a child as well as the physical well-being.
- Ensure that there are plans in place for emergencies such as fire, floods, and wind damage.
- Supply meals for the hungry and housing for the homeless.
- Engage in on-going, caregiving ministry, such as Stephen Ministry.[5]
- Make available the location and equipment needed for the group pursuit of creative interests. One church has a quilting group. Another has a workshop with donated woodworking tools. Another church provides an auto mechanic shop once a month for minor repairs. One church that is near high-rise apartments has a potting room and the opportunity for garden lovers to work in the church garden. Another arranged for a vacant lot to be turned into a shared garden. These creative interests often fill a void for persons who are lacking community after a full life in the work world.

When such facilities and programs are in place, even persons who do not need them currently will recognize the caring attitude of the congregation and know that the church will be a safe place when they do have such a need. The word *sanctuary* in reality means "a safe place." We must create sanctuary for people who need caring.

Forgiveness

If we are nothing else in the church, we should certainly be a place of forgiveness. For without forgiveness we cannot even stand in the shadow of Christ. We shy away from forgiveness because we are afraid of being nosey about other people's affairs. Yet we do not have to know about others to forgive them. The forgiving spirit is the core of relationship, and that spirit is a mark of the hospitable church.

Anyone who has been in a church for many years has certainly had an experience of major hurt or disagreement among the members. Unless healing takes place, this cancer of emotional unrest can grow into a split in the congregation. The healing power of forgiveness and using a discernment process for decision making can help in such situations. (See page 39 for suggested steps in discernment.)

Each worship service should have some form of confession and assurance of forgiveness. There are several from our early church heritage, usually printed in our hymnals. But from time to time we need some fresh, new litanies or prayers, even if it is simply a response such as asking the worshipers to turn to a neighbor and say, "If I have said or done anything that hurt or offended you, I ask your forgiveness."

A Litany of Reconciliation

Loving God, we come seeking reconciliation.

Guide us as we confess our sins.

When Jesus rode triumphantly into Jerusalem, his followers

joined a crowd crying, "Hosanna." Five days later, they denied him.

May God forgive us for the many ways we follow the crowd and deny our faith.

For the times we have been too busy to seek God's guidance in bringing reconciliation to the world...

(Offer silent or spoken prayers.)

For the times we have watched from afar rather than supporting people in trouble or advocating for the oppressed...

(Offer silent or spoken prayers.)

For the times we have run after pleasure and possessions at the expense of our brothers and sisters in need...

(Offer silent or spoken prayers.)

For the times we have avoided taking a stand on a complex issue because we have feared rejection...

(Offer silent or spoken prayers.)

For the times we have lived at enmity with the earth, wasting resources and leaving scarred crosses where forested hillsides once flourished...

(Offer silent or spoken prayers.)

For the times when, like Peter, we have denied Jesus rather than witnessing to the faith and working with others in conscientious action...

(Offer silent or spoken prayers.)

May God hear our prayers of confession, and our pleas for God's reconciling presence.

Let us receive with joy God's generous mercy and forgiveness. May God plant in us seeds of reconciliation and peace. Amen.[6]

Healing

One of the most absorbing questions about life in periods of crisis is the one we cannot help but ask: WHY? Sometimes there is a definite consequential answer, but very often it remains a mystery.

Leslie Weatherhead, in his little book *The Will of God*, defines God's will in three parts: "The *intentional will* of God means the way in which God pours himself out in goodness, such as the true father longs to do for his son."[7]

Created in the image of God, we were intentionally given free will "because man's free will creates circumstances of evil that cut across God's plan...there is a will within the will of God, or what I call 'the *circumstantial will* of God.'"[8]

Weatherhead does not leave us with the empty thought that it's "just that way"! He suggests that we can use the circumstantial will of God and continue to develop our understanding and relationship with God. We know that nothing can happen that will finally defeat God because of God's omnipotence. But we must follow God's guidance in working to fulfill the original plan, and then we will accomplish the *ultimate will* of God.[9] God will continue to bring about the ultimate will, even when the original will has been thwarted.

We cannot always know the why, but we can be assured that God is with us throughout the crisis, crying tears right along with us.

We must also cry with others, just as the little boy who spent some time next door with his elderly neighbor whose wife had recently died. The old man was sitting on the front porch crying when the boy arrived. He climbed up in the gentleman's lap and sat there for a period of time as his mother watched from the yard. When he returned home the mother asked what he had said to the neighbor. The little boy said, "Nothing, I just climbed up in his lap and helped him cry." We, too, must climb up in a lap and cry along with those who need healing from trauma.

In the eleventh chapter of John we read the story of Lazarus' death. In the story, Jesus learned of Lazarus' illness and pending death some time before he actually went to see the family. He could have gotten there earlier and healed Lazarus, but he waited. When he did arrive, rather than assuring Mary and Martha that he would raise their brother from the dead, he took time to sit and cry with them. Jesus affirmed the natural process of grief. Jesus helped them to cry.

St. John United Methodist Church in Kansas City had a well-loved member who was diagnosed with a serious disease. The news came as a jolt to the whole congregation, particularly to his Sunday school class. Several members of the class asked the staff for help in understanding what such suffering means and how healing might come about. From this common hurt arose a churchwide study on healing. Each adult class spent several weeks following a study manual on healing. Then members of the church who were professional doctors were asked to sit on a panel with the pastors to discuss the healing process. Finally, a task force was formed and a healing service planned. Members wrote the liturgy, and the music director wrote a special anthem for use in the service. The service was not only a healing balm for those individuals who were hurting, but it served as a uniting factor for the whole church. We sometimes need healing in ways that we are not even aware.

CHAPTER 7

Hospitality of Receiving

If you consider me a friend because of Christ, then
welcome Onesimus as you would welcome me.
Philemon 1:17 (CEV)

It was a couple of weeks before Christmas when a neighbor stopped by the house to speak with my husband about a neighborhood association matter. As I joined them on the front porch I noticed the neighbor's five-year-old daughter was sitting in the car waiting for her mom. As I approached the car my first thought, since it was close to Christmas, was to initiate a conversation about what she wanted Santa to bring her for Christmas. Then I recognized the opportunity that I have often suggested: that parents grasp the opportunity to share a new understanding of gifts. I asked the young girl, "What are you going to give your mother for Christmas?"

63

Her eyes lit up brighter than a Christmas tree! She began to share with me some of the plans she had for her mother's gifts. One of them she had made in preschool, and one she planned to buy with her own money. Then we talked about just how excited her mother would be to receive the gift. We imagined how her eyes would light up on Christmas morning when she unwrapped the package. Receiving a gift is as important as giving one.

Receiving Gifts

My mother had a hard decision to make when she was a young bride during the depression. She told me that my dad had selected some dress fabric as a gift, and she had thought it too expensive. She took it back to the store and exchanged it, but she felt that thereafter my father had not been confident in purchasing a gift on his own. He had felt rejected because his choice of a gift had not been affirmed by her acceptance.

Jesus taught us that receiving gifts is important when he cheerfully received the gift of oil from a woman even though the disciples wanted to sell it and give the money to the poor. You can read this story in Matthew 26, Mark 14, and John 12. Jesus recognized the woman's gift as an affirmation.

Our attitudes and responses to gifts are as important as the gifts themselves. We usually make a big fuss over the gifts of children, even if it's something we'd prefer not to wear in public. But we forget that an adult may have special feelings about a gift that he or she gives. I recall two items that I received as wedding gifts that came with special feelings attached. One was a gift from my mother. It was an expensive towel set that I recalled had been a gift to her. A matching towel set was something we never had in our home, and she knew that I had commented on how much I liked it when she had received it as a gift. It was also green plaid, my favorite color. Mother had put the gift aside, saving it for a year so that I could have it for our first apartment. I treasured that towel set until it became so threadbare that it no longer held water. I'm not sure I ever expressed my appreciation for it as fully as I should have.

The other gift was from a friend in college. She lived across the hall from me in the dorm, and one thing that she taught me was that selection of gifts should take into consideration not only the interests and personality of the receiver, but a bit of the giver too. She shopped cautiously for gifts, and I knew that she had considered both my husband and myself when I opened her gift. In the box lay a lovely vase with green leaves (again my favorite color) and four water glasses with pheasants on them. My husband loved to hunt pheasant. The ironic part is that this gift not only represented our interests, but a real sacrifice on the part of my friend! She had found the glasses, of all places, in the grocery aisles of a nearby store, but they were each filled with peanut butter, not the best brand. She had eaten four glassfuls of mediocre peanut butter in order to give us the gift of pheasant glasses. We used those glasses for many years before they all met their destiny as pieces swept into the dustpan, about the time that my friend died of cancer. But I will always remember the giver and her sacrifice of eating mediocre peanut butter!

Sometimes we ignore the gift of words. How many times, when someone has complimented you on a piece of clothing, have you said something like, "Oh, it's not much, just something I picked up at the store." Or if we are commended on something that we have made or done we say, "Oh, anyone could have done that. It's nothing!" We pass such statements off as being humble, but it is not humility at all. In fact, when we look at it from the point of view of the person giving the compliment, our statements are actually degrading. If we belittle something that someone has complimented us on then we are in essence saying, "Your opinion is not worth anything. You don't know what you are talking about!"

In order to be hospitable in receiving we must always look at giving as an act that stems from the heart. Certainly, there are some people who see giving as an obligation to be carried out and no more. But the way that we accept the gift, even if it is not given with heart, may present a different view of giving to someone else.

Receiving Care

Somewhere along the line we have forgotten that God put us on this earth to be in community with others. In Genesis 2:18 we read, "Then the LORD God said, 'It is not good that the man should be alone; I will make him a helper as his partner'"(CEV). And so God created us in community. Created in God's own image, we have an innate need to be with other people and with God. Where did we lose that knowledge? When did we decide that it is better to do things on our own, rejecting the help of others? Did it start when we learned to mount a horse and ride off in our own direction? Was it when we invented machines that enabled us to live a distance from friends and associates? Was it when we became so specialized in our careers that we lost our need to pool resources? Whatever caused it, we now isolate ourselves in cubicles, whether at home or on the road.

There are many occasions when my husband and I have been reminded of our dependence on community. We have one reminder hanging in our home now. Some years ago we built a small log home in the north Georgia mountains. We met another couple building a log home nearby. When they saw the door that Sam had made for our home, they wanted him to make one for them. The woman offered to exchange a quilt for the door. We have moved several times since we left the mountains, and our log cabin belongs to someone else now. We have not even kept contact with these friends, but that quilt has been Sam's pride for a dozen years. He appreciates every stitch that our friend put into the fabric. The circles and curves of the stitching remind us both that God placed us in community. We must remain open to receive from others if we are to survive emotionally.

I have recently been reading a book, *Ghosts from the Nursery,*[10] which tells about the importance of the emotional care given to children during the first three years of life. Many studies indicate that what happens during those years sets a disposition of caring or violence. Right in the middle of those important first years we encounter the "terrible twos." We have lauded and labeled this natural process of independence and allowed it to become the foundation for personality formation instead of a stepping stone. We allow our children to be "in charge" before they have the tools to handle that responsibility.

Even when we, as adults, take on the caring role, we sometimes mix it up with dominating others. We are so accustomed to being in charge, making sure that everybody is happy and taken care of. This puts us in a position of playing God. If we are always giving and doing for others, then we feel we have power over them. When we reject others caring for us, we deprive that person of the joy of caring.

There is an old, old story that tells of a wise man who traveled about a country that was in the midst of a drought and had no grain. One day he met a widow and asked her to cook some bread for him to eat. She told him that she only had a small amount of flour, and that she was on her way to cook up that flour into bread that would be the last meal that she and her son would have, because they would then starve to death without food. The wise man told her to go ahead and cook up the bread, but to give him some of the bread and then her supply of flour would not run out before the rain fell and the country was again blessed with wheat. The woman cleaned out her cupboard in faith, and the wise man's prediction came true. This wise man's name was Elijah, and he spoke for God. You can read the story in the seventeenth chapter of 1 Kings.

Sometimes we only learn to receive after we have reached the bottom of our flour jar and cannot take care of ourselves. In reality, our hands must be emptied in order to receive. They may be emptied by circumstances beyond our control, or we may learn to empty them ourselves from time to time. Only by emptying our hands can we move into a receiving mode. And when we are in the receiving mode we give others strength.

Because of the wisdom in the story of Elijah, the tradition of an empty chair rose among the Jewish community. At the celebration of Passover an empty chair is set at the table, just in case Elijah should come to be with the family.

Receiving Others

In Zimbabwe there is a custom of hospitality where a family moves out of their home in order to allow a guest to have the home in privacy. When Godwin Hlatshwayo was a boy in Zimbabwe, a missionary came to visit the village. According to the custom, Godwin's family moved into a friend's home so that the missionary could use theirs. The young boy had the responsibility and privilege of taking water for washing to the guest the next morning. He was told to stand outside the home and call out in English to the missionary, "The boy brings the water for my lord." He practiced and practiced, and that morning he set out with the water, excited to serve the guest. When he stepped in front of the house he called out, "The lord brings the water for my boy." To Godwin's surprise and embarrassment, the missionary was very agitated by the mistake and scolded the boy severely.[11]

The way that we receive others, mistakes and all, can make a difference in how we are received ourselves. That which we give will be returned, tapped down and running over. Jesus received a variety of persons into his intimate circle of disciples. He received as friends some of the most hated persons of his day. And when he was killed between two criminals, he received into the kingdom of God the thief who asked. Can we do less?

One area of receiving hospitality that is often overlooked is a ministry to those who have moved. Moving can be a traumatic situation, particularly for those who have lived in the same community most of their lives. In my lifetime, I have moved well over twenty times. This has placed me on location as a "stranger" in multiple situations. Even moving from one neighborhood to another within a community can create a stranger status. Growing up in a parsonage, I have always thought that my parents brainwashed me into believing that moving was fun! Knowing that a move was always in the not-too-distant future, after a couple of years in a house we began talking about what our next move might hold, what the house might be like, what sort of neighbors we might have. Consequently, because of my many moves, I am very sensitive to the feelings of those who move. I

make a point to visit persons who are new to the neighborhood and welcome them.

I've also counseled persons who have moved, tell-
ing them that their new neighbors have no real need to
get out and get acquainted with them. They already have
their own friends and their own life events. They are
comfortable in their routine or in their busy lives, and
consequently they see no need to get to know someone
else. However, the new person does have a need, and so
therefore it is the responsibility of the new person to get
out and become acquainted with the neighbors, with
the community, and to find a church that fits their family. When I'm the new person in the neighborhood I've
been known to knock on doors in order to introduce
myself, or at least to stop during a walk and talk to someone outside in the yard or someone I meet on the elevator.

I believe people who move have to reverse the normal understanding of hospitality. They must reach out
to the community and encourage hospitality. Sometimes
their actions will teach those in the community just what
hospitality is.

Perhaps this is a mission of the church. We can reach
into the neighborhood, inviting persons to take part in
some sort of session acquainting them with the community. Ask representatives of the library and other community organizations to come to the meeting and give a
brief presentation. Provide maps and telephone lists with
pertinent information. Depending on the mobility of your
neighborhood, you might hold this routinely two to four
times a year. Even if you only have four to six persons
attend, you have opened your doors of hospitality to
those two to four persons.

Melanie Rowlison has the hospitality responsibility
of the staff of St. Andrew Church in Littleton, Colorado.

She gives this definition for hospitality: *a love of strangers, creating an environment where people feel valued and cared for, welcomed, safe, and comfortable—where relationships can develop and persons are at ease, even in unfamiliar surroundings.*

That last phrase, "in unfamiliar surroundings," is the key to the hospitality of receiving.

CHAPTER 8

Hospitality of Releasing

"Go sell everything you own! Give the money to the poor, and you will have riches in heaven. Then come and be my follower."

Matthew 19:21 (CEV)

Releasing is one of the most difficult things that we must do, releasing of persons, releasing of possessions, and releasing of dreams and traditions. Yet we cannot be truly hospitable without releasing.

Releasing Dreams and Traditions

How often we block hospitality because of jealousy or fear of losing our own dreams. I recall a time when I asked someone about the status of a common friend. Immediately, the person seemed to bristle as he told me that our friend had received a promotion and assignment to a position he himself had dreamed about for years. I sensed no joy over the friend's good fortune. These two men had been good friends for several years, working in the same organization, bucking common problems. Now, the realization of one man's dream, which necessarily blocked the dream of the other, threatened to become a wedge in their friendship.

At times like this we have two choices, either to make ourselves and everyone around us miserable, or to rejoice in the good fortune of the other person, take part in the happiness, and set new dreams for ourselves. I cannot understand the commonly used term *sweet revenge*. Revenge only eats at us, creating an inner sore that never heals but grows like a cancer. There is never an end to revenge until we are all-consumed.

Because our churches become so caught up in numbers, we often think that any dream that will bring numerical growth is a gift from God, and we should pursue it. I know of a church that was convinced God had called them to expand their membership by moving to a new site and building a large physical complex. As they began to plan, every direction they turned met with some sort of obstacle. They thought they had their property sold, and the sale fell through. They located new property, and the community building commission piled up restriction upon restriction for the use of it. People in the church became divided over the decision, creating hard feelings among those who had previously worked together in ministry. Finally the governing body realized that they needed to pull back and spend some time actually discerning God's will in the matter. After several weeks of involving the whole church in a discernment process, they realized that they needed to bury the old dream and begin to dream a new one. They found their ministry in a commitment to healing and comforting those around them in their present community and thereby found healing themselves. The church has not become stagnant in numbers; in fact they continue to attract several new members a year. But they have found their ministry, and it is not in being a huge cathedral-type congregation. They were able to release their dream of numerical greatness and grasp the dream of spiritual depth in small numbers.

In my young adult years I felt that traditions held no real importance. They seemed to be cumbersome baggage to carry from generation to generation. In most dictionaries, tradition is defined as a long-established custom or practice that has the effect of an unwritten law. I find, however, that "long-established" can be a matter of months in today's world. Persons who reject traditions usually substitute the rejected one with some new tradition that they guard as preciously as others had protected the old customs and practices. They are looking for some sort of stability, some tie to the community, even a tie between the past, present, and future.

And so traditions, for tradition's sake, should not be rejected. In fact, traditions build ties; traditions bring back memories and create stability; traditions build community; traditions create identity and ownership. But there are times when we must release a tradition in order to establish a new one. Or we must release a tradition in order to create a hospitable community.

One of the problems that the Christian community faced when they began to expand their ministry outside their immediate circle of friends was how to deal with tradition. Paul faced this when he argued for the acceptance of Gentiles. There was a faction of the church that insisted that any persons who became Christian should first accept the Hebrew customs and traditions. You can read Paul's arguments in chapter 15 of Acts. Eventually, church traditions became established in the Gentile world. Over many generations the traditions of the early Roman Catholic Church became shackles to some, and many of those traditions had to be pushed aside in a new world.

As our world expanded and our mission outreach went to persons with no Judeo-Christian background, we found traditions binding us again. Now we recognize our mistake of pushing traditions that were strictly European in nature on peoples who had their own traditions and culture. Today, when we take a mission into a different culture, we find ways to spread the message of Christ through some of the local heritage and customs. We no longer force our music or clothing on those with whom we share the message. We embrace local architecture for the church buildings. We recognize manners and underlying customs as legitimate.

Today we see our world changing right before our eyes, and we recognize that we must adjust and adapt to those changes. Just as we learned that we can worship at hours other than eleven o'clock on Sundays, we are now learning that worship space can take many different forms and that music and liturgy come in more than one size.

For years, members of churches in America worshiped at 11:00 a.m. on Sundays. When a church found it necessary to change that hour, there was a cry of objection from the congregation. In researching the origin of the eleven o'clock hour, we discovered that this was established during the agricultural era, when it was necessary to hold services at this hour in order to give farmers time to milk the cows and attend to other such duties before the service hour. By understanding the origin of the tradition, many churches were able to adjust the hour successfully. We are now confronted with threats to other traditions in our worship experience.

Some churches are adding alternative services, both in times and days and also in format. By doing this, the church is exhibiting hospitality to those who do not enjoy the traditions. Many find these new approaches helpful in their spirituality. The real purpose of our worship services is to enable persons to worship God in community. If our traditions are hampering someone from worshiping God, then we are not being hospitable. God can be worshiped in many ways. Consequently we need not wait for an overflow of the seating space before adding an alternative worship service. The purpose of such an additional service should be to allow others to worship in a manner that they find most meaningful.

Traditions are important to our stability and are therefore precious to us. We feel threatened when anyone attempts to alter them. However, there are many occasions when we may need to release our stronghold on a tradition in order to accomplish a goal. These are the times when we must evaluate the importance of a tradition. The outcome of questions such as those below can help you decide whether to hold on to the tradition or to release and transform it.

- What is the origin of the tradition?
- What was the purpose of the tradition at its origin?
- Is that purpose still legitimate?
- How important is the tradition to my spiritual/emotional well-being?
- How important is the tradition to other persons' spiritual/emotional well-being? To whose?
- Does this tradition stand in the way of someone else's spiritual/emotional development?
- Can the tradition be altered with satisfaction for all concerned?
- Can a new tradition be established that will better accomplish the purpose and take the place of this one?

- Can this tradition and a new one coexist, accomplishing the purpose(s)?

Evaluations of traditions are important in any circumstance where we deal with other persons. Such evaluations help us to be more hospitable in our homes and also in our churches.

Henri Nouwen, in his book *Reaching Out,* suggests that "hospitality is not a subtle invitation to adopt the life style of the host, but the gift of a chance for the guest to find his own."[12] What a wonderful gift we have to offer to those around us! We can truly create space for others to become their own persons in Christ. That gift comes from the heart.

Releasing Our Possessions

There once was a young man who came to Jesus asking what he should do to have eternal life. Jesus recognized that this young man had a firm grip on his physical possessions and that the love for those possessions was blocking his relationship with God. Jesus tried to help him create an environment where others would feel free and cared for. He encouraged the young man to release his control over the possessions that held him captive by selling all that he had and giving the money to the poor. Sadly the young man was not able to accept this. Here is an example of someone who could not bear to release that which bound him. He could not face the release necessary to make him hospitable, and so he went away sad.

The release of possessions serves two functions. It not only helps those to whom we give our possessions, but it also helps the giver. Too often our possessions become our identity. We feel that we have earned what we have, that those possessions are extensions of self. There is nothing wrong with pride over the tangible by-products of our work. We should, however, recognize that God gave us the brains and ability to fulfill that work. Without those gifts from God we could not carry out the responsibilities of the job that enables us to draw a paycheck. The problem comes about when we center on the material achievements and let these things become our primary focus, pushing God and God's calling aside.

This is a real challenge in today's world. We are bombarded on all sides every day by challenges to buy bigger, to have more, to play the game! Merchandizing even tries to fill our need to give to others as it pushes us to buy more for ourselves. There is a jewelry store in our community that I would not frequent even if I had the money to buy their expensive products. Their advertising gimmick during one holiday season was to ask customers to bring canned goods for a food pantry and receive a 10 percent discount! I enjoy jewelry too, but if I decide to purchase an expensive diamond bracelet, I don't think I should sugar-coat the purchase by giving to a food pantry. I should acknowledge that I am buying the jewelry for myself and wrestle with God over the stewardship of my money. Gifts to a food pantry need to be true gifts, not a ticket for a discount.

Another possession that we hang onto is our possession of "busyness." Being busy has become a status symbol in our society. Hardly a conversation occurs that we don't comment on how busy we are. In the past, if someone asked, "How are you?" our response usually centered on health. Today, the usual reply to such a question is, "Keeping busy!" The cliché of the day is "Busy, busy, busy!"

Our church calendars fill every day and every night. If there is an empty slot, we rush to fill it. Are we creating a god out of our busyness? Instead of trying to plan something for everyone and something for every hour, we should create spaces and places of emptiness for our members and guests. What a hospitable mission in a rushed world, to open our libraries for quiet reading and reflection, to create a garden of butterflies and tadpoles, to create reflective spots in children's classrooms, and to become known as a place to come and find yourself since it's so easy to get lost in the world.

We are not only called to release our possessions and our busyness, but we are also called to release our hold on another person in order to create the environment for true hospitality.

Releasing People

When we look for examples of a releasing atmosphere in the Bible, Naomi is one of the first stories that comes to mind. After the death of her husband and her two sons, Naomi made preparations to return to her homeland. Her daughters-in-law, Ruth and Orpah, expected to leave their own country and go with Naomi. However, in a dramatic scene, Naomi released Ruth and Orpah. Although only Orpah took their mother-in-law up on the offer, Naomi's act was certainly one of hospitality. She allowed the young women the freedom to choose. She created an environment where the women felt valued and cared for, yet free to follow their own calling. Such hospitality probably transformed Ruth's relationship with Naomi, even though Ruth went with her into her home country. The offer of releasing on the part of Naomi created an environment where Ruth felt free to stay in her own country. Because Naomi was willing to release her daughter-in-law, Ruth's decision to stay with her had an even greater impact on the deep friendship between the two women. It could not have been so strong, and so freeing at the same time, had Naomi not taken the first step of releasing the choice to Ruth.

Although it is believed that Paul never married and did not have a child of his own, we do know that he had a parent's love for Onesimus. This young man had been a slave to Philemon before he ran away and ended up spending some time with Paul. Yet Paul exhibited hospitality when he sent a letter to Philemon, releasing Onesimus. Paul could have kept Onesimus in Rome, for he was not only a comfort but also a great help to him. However, in his letter to Philemon we read Paul's request that Onesimus be welcomed as he would welcome Paul himself. And in verse 20 of that letter Paul asks, "My dear friend and follower of Christ our Lord, please cheer me up by doing this for me" (CEV). Paul showed hospitality through releasing Onesimus, and he called on Philemon to extend hospitality by receiving the young man in the manner in which he would receive Paul.

Hospitality among family members is one of the hardest acts to achieve. This is in part because we have such a strong interest in the other family member, whether it be a child or adult, that we have difficulty releasing control. We also find our lives so busy that we don't take the time to place ourselves in the family member's shoes before we react. We come up with an immediate answer or statement without due consideration.

When my children were in high school, I discovered that any time they asked for permission to do something, my immediate reaction was no. Then later, when I thought it through, I sometimes puzzled over why I had denied the request. At that point, I felt I could not back down on my decision, so I was in conflict within myself as well as with the children. In order to force myself to take the time to think a request through from their point of view, I made a policy of not answering a request immediately. They had to give me time to think about it.

Perhaps we should visualize our family members as guests in our home and take the time to consider how we would treat them if they were our guests. It might make a difference in how we would ask them to carry out a task or how we would request appropriate behavior.

We also need to recognize that family members act out of love for one another. For example, persons who care about each other recognize how their actions affect the other person. It is simply an act of hospitality to let the person preparing a meal know whether or not you will be at the table when it is served. Leaving a message of our whereabouts or notifying the family when we expect to be late becomes a caring act instead of simply a burden placed on one member of the family by another. In all occasions, we should place ourselves in the position of the other person.

We often find it particularly hard to be hospitable about releasing our children. When children are young, we guide and direct their actions. And this is appropriate. Preschoolers and elementary children look to adults as models. This is the time when we must be advocates, pointing the way and giving direction. However, even in the midst of guiding and modeling, it is important that we release our children enough to give them options. If we do not encourage them to think for themselves, they will be lost when they are forced to do so without our help.

I recall one of the first times that I really recognized the importance of giving children the gift of thinking for themselves. I was visiting in a preschool classroom during snack time when a child accidentally tipped his juice over. My reaction, like that of many mothers, was to rush for the paper towels and instruct the child in helping me clean up. I learned a little about releasing control as I saw that the teacher watched the puddle of juice expand and simply asked the child, "What do you suppose we should do about this?"

The child looked at the juice on the floor, and then he said, "I'll get the paper towels and wipe it up so no one will fall."

After the clean-up was complete, the teacher asked, "Now, what can you do so that this won't happen again?" To which the child decided to set his cup of juice back from the edge of the table. Many adults' reaction would have been to administer a stern scolding. This might have changed the child's behavior, but only at the price of discomfort and guilt. By releasing control over the child, this teacher allowed the situation to become an opportunity for growth.

A church can help parents recognize the natural process of releasing their children by developing a support group for parents of young adult children. A service of rededication of adult children might also be considered.

Litany for Rededication of Our Children

Leader: Children are gifts from God, on loan to us for a short time. Children need the love and nurture that parents give. Their need for love is most evident when they are young, but they continue to need that love throughout their lives. In this time together we particularly remember our children who have grown.

Parent #1:   We remember the birth of a child. There was joy and excitement. It was a true miracle revealed in flesh, created by God.

ALL: **Thank you, God, for your creation that is so evident in children.**

Parent #2:   We remember the times we walked the floor at night with a child, feeling utterly helpless. There were times when we felt inadequate and had to turn to God for assurance and help.

ALL: **Thank you, God, for being there when we needed you.**

Leader: With joy we remember the occasions when, before a congregation, we released our children to God. And we remember the support that our church family gave us.

Parent #1:   We remember the Sunday school teachers who helped in the nurture of our children. Week after week, they told the stories and spread their arms with love. We remember when our children received their first Bibles. With this act we recognized again the importance of the Word in our lives.

ALL: **Thank you, God, for the caring church family.**

Parent #2:   We also recall the times that we failed to put God first in our family lives. There were times when the pressures of the world seemed so great that we found it easy to let go of that very core support that the church provides.

ALL: **Forgive us, Lord, for we are not always as strong as we would like to be.**

Leader: And now our children are grown. We have given them much. We have occasionally failed, but with faith we go forward. The time has come when we must release them into God's hands again, trusting what guidance we have given them in the past and trusting God's guidance in the future.

Parent #1: We do not desert them, for we will continue to love them and pray for them daily. We will give them support in their personal choices.

ALL: **We recognize, O God, that we cannot force our opinions on our children. They must make their choices themselves. Remind us of the opportunities to express our love, even when we do not approve of their choices.**

Parent #2: We look forward to a different type of relationship with our children. We recognize that they are adults, and we now dedicate ourselves to nurturing the adult friendships we have with our children.

ALL: **We ask that you, our Parent, guide us as we move into these new relationships with our children.**

Leader: These children came to us as infants, wholly dependent on us. They are now adults going into the world without us yet with our spirit and the Holy Spirit of the Lord.

ALL: **We release these children who are now adults to you, O God. Amen.**

From time to time a church will experience the loss of someone who has been a significant part of the community of faith. This usually brings about a period of grief, whether we recognize it or not.

Often the loss is through death, but it may also come through a move. It is important that we plan some way to release the person, recognizing the contribution that the person has made to the church and to the individual lives within the church. And a part of the therapy of such a loss is to allow the whole congregation to be a part of the planning as well as the celebration of ministry.

Whether there is a death or a move, the loss creates a void that needs to be mourned. This period of grief is doubly hard when the loss is a staff member. We have relied so heavily on the staff member that we are pulled between the need to work through our grief and the need to have someone hired for the position. Several years ago I was asked to come to a church as an interim Christian educator. The woman who had held that position for many years was leaving, and the church was considering a reconfiguration of the position. The pastor said, "We just need someone for about six months to help us grieve and to keep the wheels turning." I thought how wise of that church to acknowledge the perfectly normal grieving process of this situation. Some of our churches have done a good job in supplying interim pastors, but I had never known of a conscious hiring of an interim person for another staff position.

Ties are naturally made in the church, particularly when we work with a staff person over an extended period of time. Sometimes the loss is like pulling a life support system. Yet we do not allow a grieving period. The new staff member that is hired then comes on board expecting to "do great things for the Lord" and meets a blank wall of mourners. The problem is that it's hard to recognize them as mourners. They are usually just seen as folks who don't want to change. In reality, the resistance to change is a form of denial, as we try to hold onto what has been taken away. This is all a natural part of the mourning process, which, if not dealt with, can become hostility, eating at the heart of the church family and creating an inhospitable environment.

Releasing Status

In our society today, status is sometimes our life-blood. I recall a father who would not allow his son to join the wrestling team but insisted that he play basketball. Now, in that small community wrestling was a sport of little importance. The real pride of the community was in the basketball team! Everyone turned out for the games. The boy was fairly good at both sports, but his heart was in wrestling. However, his father sought a boost to his own status through his son's participation in the basketball team. He wanted to be able to boast about *his* son who was out on the floor shooting baskets.

The driver's license also serves as a status symbol, particularly for teenagers and senior adults. For teens it is a status of being "old enough," and for senior adults it is a status of being "young enough." Several churches have developed a service for dedication of the driver's license for their youth, even accompanying it with training on the stewardship of the car.

Few churches recognize the opportunity to help older adults release the independence that the driver's license signifies. There comes a time in everyone's life, if we live long enough, when it is no longer safe to drive. That is a hard point to acknowledge. By creating a celebration of the person's past driving ministry, we can help the church continue to be a place where people are welcomed and feel cared for.

Our Ministry of Driving

A litany for use in a dedication of the driver's license. The licenses may be placed in a basket for dedication and lifted up during the leader's closing statement.

Leader: We recognize driving as an important skill in today's world.

Youth #1: We use the skill to visit friends and relatives who live a distance from ourselves.

All: For this we thank you, Lord.

Youth #2: We use the skill to bring food and supplies to our homes and churches.

All: For this we thank you, Lord.

Youth #1: We use the skill to get medical help when necessary.

All: For this we thank you, Lord.

Youth #2: We use the skill to help meet the needs of other people.

All: For this we thank you, Lord.

Leader: We acknowledge, O God, that there have been times when we have not used this skill to your glory.

Adult #1: When we have driven too fast for road and personal conditions,

All: We ask your forgiveness, Lord.

Adult #2: When we have recklessly or thoughtlessly endangered the lives of others in the way that we drive,

All: We ask your forgiveness, Lord.

Adult #1: When we have not insisted that those driving with us exercise safety measures,

All: We ask your forgiveness, Lord.

Adult #2: When we have ignored or postponed maintenance procedures or the mechanical warnings of our cars,

All:	**We ask your forgiveness, Lord.**
Leader:	We dedicate ourselves to using this skill of driving for your glory.
Youth #1:	Help us to remain alert to all that is happening around us as we drive.
All:	**We pray for your guidance, Lord.**
Adult #1:	Remind us of the responsibility that we have for others who share the road when we sit behind the wheel.
All:	**We pray for your guidance, Lord.**
Youth #2:	Help us remember to exercise courtesy to others and make the roads a hospitable place to be.
All:	**We pray for your guidance, Lord.**
Adult #2:	Bring to our minds ways that we can be of service to others with this skill.
All:	**We pray for your guidance, Lord.**
Leader:	Lord, we know that our drivers' licenses are a permit that the state gives with permission to use this skill. We recognize that along with that permit comes responsibility to follow the laws set by the state.
	We now bring these licenses before you, reminding us that everything that we do in our Christian life, including our driving, is an act of worship to you. With these licenses as symbols of ourselves, we now offer this skill of driving to you. May we use the skill to your glory.
	We ask you to give us the strength and courage to resist those who urge us to use our driving skills in unsafe ways; keep us alert and

aware of what is happening around us; and calm us when we are in a hurry or when we must make choices.

All: **Help us to use our driving skills as gifts for good and not instruments of harm. Give us guidance to show hospitality on the road. Amen.**[13]

Celebration of a Driving Ministry

A litany to be used when it is necessary for a person to relinquish a driver's license. That person speaks where it is indicated as "honoree."

Leader: We come together in a happy celebration. We celebrate the gift of driving and our opportunity to use that skill in the service of our Lord.

Honoree: I thank God for the opportunity to use the skill of driving for these years.

Leader: This servant of God has found many occasions in which to serve through the use of an automobile. There are people here who can attest to this ministry.

(At this point, persons who care to will briefly mention occasions when the honoree served God through the skill of driving. These may include delivering food to those in need, coming to planning meetings, bringing family or friends to church, visiting in the hospital, and other such occasions.)

Leader: We lift up these special times of service. May those who benefited from this able ministry go on to serve others.

Honoree: It has been a joy to serve God in these ways. I now look forward to new avenues of service.

Leader: This example of service through the gift of
           driving will always stand as a model, but we
           celebrate with you in your new ventures of
           service. As your sisters and brothers in Christ
           we commit to assisting you where we can, so
           that you may continue to serve the Lord.

           Let us pray:

           We lay before you, our God, all of the
           ministries that this servant of yours has brought
           about with the skill of driving. We celebrate
           this today.

           We also ask for your guidance in the future
           as new avenues of ministry are charted. Help
           us to be a support and to assist in whatever
           way that we can. We dedicate our service to
           you together. Amen.

CHAPTER 9

Hospitality of Celebrating

Sing praises to the LORD! Tell about his miracles.
Celebrate and worship his holy name with all your heart.
Psalm 105:2–3 (CEV)

There is a joy of living that bubbles over and shows
through all of life when we celebrate. Too often we feel
that we can't celebrate because we don't have the proper
equipment or because we are afraid of doing it wrong.
There are many forms of celebration. Some are formal
and some quite informal. For some we plan over a long
period of time. With those, the anticipation and planning takes on a celebration of its own. And then there
are spontaneous times of celebration.

Our church has many members who leave our community during the summer for an extended time. I recall
one "routine" midweek supper when I walked through

the door and saw several of our members whom I'd not seen for four months because of their extended vacations. The delight and excitement, hugs and laughter disrupted the routine meal, but that was a time of celebrating! Those spontaneous times of joy are the baguettes that surround larger celebrations, adding brilliance to our lives.

Whether planned or spontaneous, large, elaborate occasions or small, intimate happenings, celebration is the blossom of hospitality.

Why Celebrate?

From the beginning of the world there have been celebrations. In Genesis we read that after each movement of creation, God stepped back to celebrate, saying, "That's good!" This story of creation was handed down from family to family by oral tradition over many centuries. The manner in which the story is told certainly lets us know that celebration has been a part of life from the beginning, and it indicates God's affirmation of celebration. Jesus took part in celebrations and even came to the host's rescue during a wedding, as recorded in John 2:1–12.

Celebrations not only give us joy over an occasion, but they affirm accomplishments, relationships, and life passages. In 2 Samuel 6:11–15, David led the procession to bring the ark of the covenant into the new city. His celebration was so great that he expressed his joy in dance.

One of my favorite Bible stories is the celebration that King Solomon planned upon completion of the temple. With great ceremony, the ark of the covenant, along with the other objects that reminded them of God's presence, was once again moved. This time it was moved into the new building, which had taken thirteen years to build (1 Kings 8, and 2 Chronicles 7).

There are other occasions of celebration in our biblical heritage. According to the book of Ezra, after the period of exile, the people returned to Jerusalem and rebuilt the city wall. Nehemiah organized a great celebration at the completion of the wall, complete with singers, cymbals, small harps, and other stringed instruments. It must have been an occasion of double joy, for completing the wall was not only an accomplishment in itself, but it was a recognition of what they had gone through in exile and how they had rebounded as a community of believers, working as a team to rebuild the wall.

These Old Testament occasions were well planned and of mammoth proportions. However, the spontaneous response of the people along the path of Jesus' entry into Jerusalem (Matthew 21, Mark 11, Luke 19, and John 12) carried just as much joy. According to Luke's retelling of the story, when the Pharisees objected and asked Jesus to make the disciples stop shouting, he said, "If they keep quiet, these stones will start shouting" (Luke 19:40 CEV). There was no way to restrain the celebration!

Of course, there was also an unplanned celebration when the disciples realized that Jesus was no longer dead, and the excitement continued to mount until it exploded among his followers on Pentecost, when about three thousand persons believed and were baptized. This celebration turned God's kingdom into a "kindom," binding all of the people who believed into a community, which we now know as the church.

Planning a Celebration

When planning a celebration, there are two primary considerations: the reason and the people. Let's consider first the reason.

Too many people today celebrate primarily for one purpose, to satisfy self. This may be something as simple as looking for a "good time," or it may be in order to make the person feel important. We have become caught up in chasing false rainbows. We feel that if we create just the right atmosphere with just the right ingredients we will find that special rainbow of happiness. We forget that true joy comes from within. And a true celebration begins within. When, within ourselves, we recognize the joy of an occasion, an accomplishment, or a relationship, then that exultation naturally comes forth in celebration. We may frame it with plans, or we may let it bloom spontaneously, but the true purpose behind such a celebration springs from within.

I have been a part of many groundbreakings over the course of my years in the church. With interest I have reflected on those events and recognized some distinct differences. Inevitably the ones that have been poorly attended were occasions where the congregation never caught the vision. In most cases the building was primarily dreamed and planned by one person or a small contingency of the members, and the congregation did not feel true ownership.

I recall one occasion where the pastor felt that the challenge to build should not be presented to the congregation until the plans were well in place. Although there were legitimate needs that the building would fill, the congregation did not see those needs because they were blinded by an impression that something was forced upon them. This did not create a hospitable atmosphere. It did not create spaces where people felt welcomed and cared for. Sadly, that congregation never felt a part of the celebration. Those who appeared for the groundbreaking stood on the sidelines, and the celebration at the completion of the building seemed to them to be just another ho-hum experience. They could not truly celebrate because the seed of excitement had not been planted early and was not nurtured throughout the process. If the leaders had first enabled the congregation to dream a bit about the church's ministry and to envision various ways to accomplish the dream, then the recognition of the need for such a building would have emerged naturally, and the congregation would have been behind it wholeheartedly. The finished building was used for many meetings and educational purposes, but it was forever referred to as "their building."

On the flip side, I remember the overflowing of excitement in another church when we all stood around a backhoe as it made its first cut into the ground. Cheers of celebration rose in unison! We had each brought our own shovel from home, and as we tossed a shovelful of dirt, we were given a sticker to put on the handle commemorating the occasion. Even the children were given small plastic shovels of their own, and before the morning was over each child (and many of the adults) had spent some time in the shallow ditch that the backhoe dug, emerging with dirt from head to toe. Praises were sung and prayers were given. Inconveniences during the building phase were met with smiles, and everyone dreamed of new classrooms and extended meeting space. The difference here was that the whole church had a mission, and that mission could be accomplished by completing the building. The building was not being erected simply for the sake of a building, and everyone knew this.

And so the underlying reason for celebration within a church is mission, and if we are truly committed to God as individuals, then the underlying reason for us to celebrate is also mission, our mission as we see God calling us. I have a great Christian friend who often gives parties and claims that one of her favorite things to do is "partying." However, any time you are with her you recognize Christ shining through in everything that she does. This comes about in an unobtrusive way. She creates a space where people are welcome and feel cared for. Celebration happens, whether she has planned it as a party or not.

When you stop and think about it, isn't this what Jesus did when he celebrated Passover with his disciples in the upper room? Passover is a celebrative meal in the Hebrew religion. If you ever have the opportunity to celebrate it in a Jewish home you will recognize that, although it has serious elements, it certainly does celebrate the release of captive slaves in a very festive way. It is thought through ahead of time. The food is well planned and prepared with care. There are candles on the table, and there is an empty chair always available. When we read Mark 14, we see Jesus as one who has made preparations ahead with the householder for a room to be prepared and ready for this celebration. His act of washing the disciples' feet in John 13 was a caring act that set the tone for the evening meal. We sometimes look on this story with a solemn attitude because we know of Jesus' arrest and crucifixion. But for the disciples it must have been a celebration—a very hospitable celebration!

The other consideration in planning a celebration is the people. Although the reason for the celebration will somewhat determine the people, it is important that we recognize that the people will make a difference in the success or failure of the celebration. This does not mean that we should be prejudiced about whom we invite, but perhaps that we should be certain that the persons invited are prepared to be a part of the celebration. Let's again consider the church that had an unsuccessful groundbreaking. For this event, the right people were invited, but they had not been prepared ahead of time. They were not ready for such a celebration. Preparation is the key ingredient.

There are many occasions for celebration that we often overlook. Perhaps we should consider reinstating some sort of celebration for various "rites of passage" in our churches. Some of these are already in place but simply need to be recognized as celebrations. Here is a list to begin with. You may think of others.

- Engaged couples
- Weddings and anniversaries
- Birthdays
- Dedication of an apartment
- Dedication of a home
- Expectant parents
- Births and adoptions
- Dedication or baptism of infants
- Beginning of school and/or middle and high school
- Bible presentation
- Believer baptism
- Confirmation
- Graduation (high school and college)
- Begin college
- First job
- New job/promotion
- Becoming a grandparent
- Retirement
- Memorial services/celebrations

In Worship

When I first attended a contemporary worship service in our church, I found it less meaningful to me than my usual traditional service. As I looked around the room I recognized that many of the persons seemed to be experiencing a time of spiritual awakening. Later, as I talked with a woman who is active in the contemporary worship, I mentioned the fact that repeating the same phrase in a praise song over and over again did not help me worship. Thankfully, she felt comfortable enough to explain to me that for her the repetition was actually a very worshipful experience. It enabled her to worship in the same way that a mantra or chant might help other people. This made me realize that each of us worships in different ways, and we must create opportunities for each person to find meaningful ways to worship.

Malcolm Goldsmith has written a book on exploring spirituality for different personalities. In *Knowing Me Knowing God*, he says that three-quarters of the general population are thought to be people whose preference is for worship that is concrete and applicable to everyday life.[14] However, Goldsmith states that in his experience in churches he has found the leadership to be primarily "intuitives" or persons who enjoy a more abstract and philosophical approach to worship. It is no wonder, then, that our general population comes to church and feels rejected because the type of worship does not help them to grow spiritually. In fact, often they are completely lost in our traditional services with symbols and rituals that they don't even understand. We no longer have the freedom of thinking that there is only one way to worship. We must encompass many ways and provide those opportunities.

In the past centuries we looked at worship style and religion in one context. Even when we went into new cultures, spreading our understanding of God, we insisted that the style of worship parallel our own. I often wonder if the people we were trying to reach felt like fish being forced to walk on dry land. In more recent years we have recognized the importance of offering God but allowing persons to worship God in a manner that is meaningful to them according to their own culture. As we move into the new millennium, we are recognizing that people within our own culture also need the option of finding ways that best help them worship God, even if it is quite different from the ways that we normally worship.

At the same time, it is important to recognize that changing worship styles must not be pushed upon persons who have found the traditional worship meaningful to them throughout their lives. Change must not come about simply for the sake of change. It is every bit as legitimate for these persons to continue to have their methods of worship available as it is for new persons to have new forms of worship.

What does this tell us about being a hospitable church? How can we go about fashioning worship experiences that meet the needs of a variety of persons? Perhaps we need to school ourselves in a variety of worship forms, introducing them to the congregation at various points, giving individuals opportunities to use their praising hands and voices in different ways.

CHAPTER 10

United in Mission

A body isn't really a body, unless there is more than one part. It takes many parts to make a single body.
1 Corinthians 12:19–20 (CEV)

If there is anything that presents our churches as inhospitable, it is the discord that often goes on between the members and various leaders. Since Christians are not "little Christs" but actually persons who often go wrong but continue to try to *follow* Christ, then we can expect some discord. But our attitudes and our goals should come from one central base, that of sharing Christ with others.

Hospitality is the heart of sharing Christ. We might look at it as a form of evangelism. Or perhaps I should say it the other way around. For years, I shied away from the word evangelism. My understanding of evangelism was akin to door-to-door hounding of people about their salvation. In recent years I have come to recognize that we practice some form of evangelism in our lives every day, whether we realize it or not. We share and act out our values. We welcome people into our homes and churches; we treat others with the love that we know comes from God.

We cannot departmentalize our lives, and we cannot departmentalize the ministries of the church. For generations we have divided our church life into little categories, each group defining the limits of their responsibility and protecting that area of the church. Consequently, education was not allowed to offer suggestions to evangelism on ways to nurture and spread the message. Evangelism could not help worship create meaningful experiences for people new to Christianity. Missions were given financial support but otherwise left to accomplish their own thing without realizing that the nurturing in education and the outreach in evangelism are parts of mission. And the trustees and finance committee held the purse strings for it all, judiciously guarding every cent for fear of bankruptcy, not aware of their important role in the extension of Christ into the community and the world.

The church moving into the twenty-first century must operate with a common purpose or mission statement. Any church that does not do this will be left shattered behind closed doors, decaying from within. It takes all parts of the body of Christ to bring about a welcoming and hospitable church. And those parts function best when working together toward a common goal.

Jesus commanded his disciples in the last verses of the book of Matthew: "Go therefore and make disciples of all nations, baptizing them in the name of the Father and of the Son and of the Holy Spirit, and teaching them to obey everything that I have commanded you. And remember, I am with you always, to the end of the age" (Matthew 28:19–20, NRSV).

If this is our primary mission, then we must develop ways to reach that mission as a whole congregation. We must meet the challenge to become a hospitable church, caring for others and worshiping God in a world of self-worshiping people.

Study Guide

This study guide is not divided into sessions purposefully. If you are studying this independently, work with the study materials along with each chapter. If you are preparing to lead a group in this study, pick and choose the elements that your particular group needs to study.

You may want to open each study session with one of the hymns suggested below. These were chosen because they reflect a challenge to answer God's call, ways that we can welcome others, the universality of God, or asking God to guide and direct us. You may have other hymns in those themes that your group knows.

The prayers are only suggestions or guides. Tailor your prayers to your group and certainly include any prayer concerns in a prayer sometime during the session. You may use a prayer anywhere you wish in the session. Sometimes it is appropriate to have a prayer after a specific discussion instead of just having "bookend" prayers at the beginning and ending of a session. Most of the prayers below leave us with a challenge and would certainly be appropriate as a "sending forth" prayer at the close.

Each participant should have a copy of the book to read during the study.

(As you begin this study, write a definition of hospitality as you see it. At the close of your study, write a new definition of hospitality and compare the two.)

Hymns

"A Charge to Keep I Have"
"Bless Be the Tie That Binds"
"Christ for the World We Sing"
"Go, Make of All Disciples"
"God of Grace and God of Glory"
"God of Many Names"
"Help Us Accept Each Other"
"Here I Am, Lord (I, the Lord of Sea and Sky)"
"Let There Be Peace on Earth"
"Lord, Speak to Me, That I May Speak"
"Lord, You Give the Great Commission"
"Pass It On"
"Where Charity and Love Prevail"
"Spirit of the Living God"

Prayers

Dear God, although we are many and varied, you still love us all. Give us the recognition of that love and help us to pass it on to others. Amen

Giver of Life, help us to recognize the needs of others as they move through life. Show us ways that we can welcome them into our lives and into our church. Amen.

Guide of Life, make us conscious of ways that we exhibit our love for you. Be the guide of our words and our actions. Amen.

Oh Great Healer, we come to you for comfort, and we ask that you give us the strength to be comforter and healer for others. Make us aware of those who are in need of your healing power. Amen.

Our Mentor Christ, we pray that we will follow your example of service. May we continually look beyond our needs and recognize the many opportunities that you lay before us for service to others. May we see that our faith not only looks toward you but also reaches out to those around us. Amen.

O Lord of us all, there are so many things that we value, some of them for good reason and some simply because we find them to be of comfort to us. Help us to weed through the many traditions we hold dear. Help us to recognize any that are stumbling blocks for others. Give us strength to remove or alter those blocks so that each person can experience your love. Amen.

Power of the Universe, we relinquish our own power and turn it over to you. We want to open our hearts in hospitality to others. Help us in our self-centeredness. Expand our horizons. And may we find the joy in sharing your loving embrace with all. Amen.

Chapter 1–Gift from Birth

- If you have ever taken the Myers-Briggs Type Indicator, compare your test outcome to the suggestions of ways that personality and hospitality parallel.
- Name persons who exhibit a true attitude of hospitality from the heart.
- Recall an act of hospitality you have received from someone you did not know during the past week.
- What experiences have you had with hospitality when visiting a church?

Chapter 2–Biblical Models of Hospitality

- Discuss the differences in the hospitality of a hotel and the hospitality of a home. How does the hospitality of a church differ from either of these?

- What are some characteristics of true hospitality?
- Look up these biblical references:

  Genesis 19
  Genesis 23
  Exodus 2
  Joshua 2:1–16
  Luke 10:38–42

- Which of the above references show the following four characteristics of hospitality and the last characteristic, which is a false hospitality?

  (1) Crosses cultural tradition of treatment of women.

  (2) Offered in the face of fear.

  (3) Expects nothing in return.

  (4) Welcomes those normally outside religious conver sation into such.

  (5) Does harm to someone else.

Chapter 3–Hospitality of Welcoming

- Look around your home and find indications of welcome that might be recognized by others.
- In what ways do you allow others to be welcomed by making them a part of your family?
- List the persons you encountered during the day yesterday, both face-to-face and casually.
- Go back through the list of persons and make a note of how you welcomed them "as if they were Christ."
- We cannot know how to care for others without getting to know them. What are some ways to get to know other people in your neighborhood, in your church, and in your community?
- Using the list on pp. 18 and 19, discuss the exterior welcome of your church. How can it be improved?

- Read the scenario on p. 20. Using the reflections on the pages that follow the scenario, make notes on how your church can make changes in order to be more welcoming:
  - in the parking lot
  - in the nursery
  - in the classrooms
  - with name tags
  - in the sanctuary
  - with informational materials
  - in other ways

Chapter 4—Hospitality of Speaking and Listening

- Review the various images of God mentioned on p. 29. Think of additional images that are suggested in the Bible. Discuss which (besides the traditional father and shepherd) is your favorite image of God.
- Sing the Doxology, using the word "God" in place of the pronouns.
- Read the words of Jesus in Mark 8:14–21 out loud, using these different emotions in your voice:
  - weariness
  - anger
  - compassion or pity
- List body language that is hospitable. List body language that is inhospitable.
- Recall a recent church meeting that you attended. Which of the bulleted items on pp. 39–40 might have been used to make it more hospitable?
- Look at your church worship bulletin and point out any times for private listening to God. If there are none, where can such time be placed?

Chapter 5–Hospitality of Serving

- What are some ways that you can gift others with the opportunity to serve without pushing it on them?

- What opportunities for service have you taken advantage of in the past week? What opportunities have you let slip by you?

- List ways that you have been affirmed for your leadership in the church.

- List other ways to affirm leaders in your church.

- Survey the number of ministries beyond your church where your church members are serving (such as hospital volunteer, Habitat for Humanity, etc.).

- Discuss times at your church when food is served. Reflect on "Spreading the Table" on pp. 49–52 and discuss how your hospitality around the table can be improved.

Chapter 6–Hospitality of Comforting and Healing

- Affirmation and encouragement are forms of comforting. How do you affirm and encourage your church staff members? How does your church affirm and encourage those in its teaching ministry? How do you affirm and encourage other volunteers?

- Read through the possible opportunities for comforting in crisis listed on pp. 57–58. Which of these is your church offering? Are there others on the list or that you can think of that your church might offer?

- Recall a specific time when there was a major misunderstanding among members of your church or of a church you know. How was the misunderstanding handled? How might it have been handled better?

- Review the steps on discernment listed on p. 39.

- Review the litany of reconciliation on p. 59. Can this be used in a Sunday service, maybe during Brotherhood Week in February or World Order Sunday in May?
- Review the information on Leslie Weatherhead's book *The Will of God* as presented on pp. 60–61. In what circumstances might you find this most helpful?

Chapter 7–Hospitality of Receiving

- Read Matthew 26:6–13. How does the story illustrate hospitality from the giver's point of view (the woman) and the receiver's (Jesus)?
- What gifts have you most appreciated in the past?
- When have you received a note of appreciation or some other form of thank-you that made you know that your gift was received with the love intended?
- How might your church encourage parents to help their children develop a new attitude about gift giving and receiving?
- The growing evidence that a tendency toward violence is determined by attitudes during early childhood emphasizes the importance of the first three years of a child's life. (See p. 67.) How can your church improve your ministry to young children and their parents?
- How can you or your church reach out to persons who are new in your community? (See pp. 69–70.)

Chapter 8–Hospitality of Releasing

- Review the manner in which you treat other family members. (See pp. 81–83.) How can you release some of your control over family members? What choices can you offer them?

- Review the "Litany for Rededication of Our Children" on p. 84 and consider how it might be used or adapted.
- Do you know of a church that is small but in exciting ministry? If not, talk with churches in your area and find one that you might visit. Talk with members of that church asking them what they appreciate about their church and discover some of the ways they are in mission.
- List traditions in your church such as the hour or order of worship, role of the pastor's wife, use or restriction of a room, mode of dress, and so on. Use the questions on pp. 77–78 to consider the wisdom of holding onto or releasing each tradition. (If you are studying this with several persons, you may wish to divide into groups for this.)
- List status symbols in society and discuss the consequences of releasing each of these.
- Read the first paragraph on p. 80. Look at your church calendar. Are there opportunities for persons to "find themselves" in our busy world? How might you develop such opportunities in your church? (These might include a quiet garden, prayer room, prayer path, quiet times in worship, etc.)

Chapter 9–Hospitality of Celebrating

- Review the spontaneous times of celebration in your life. In the life of your church.
- List opportunities for celebration that might be coming up in your church in the next year or two. Be sure that the list includes those that are more routine than founding anniversaries and new buildings. How might these be marked? What sort of preparation and groundwork will each need?

- Review the list of "rites of passage" celebrations on p. 99 and expand the list.

- How can you celebrate some of these rites of passage in your own life and with your family?

- What on this list of rites of passage does your church now celebrate? Which ones might you consider celebrating?

- Look at the two driving celebrations in the previous chapter (pp. 88 and 90) and consider how they may be used in your church.

- Review the section "In Worship" on pp. 100–101. How does your church meet the needs of persons who need varying worship styles?

Chapter 10–United in Mission

- What is the function of the evangelism committee in your church?

- Read pp. 103–105. How can your church committees cooperate in order to bring about Christ's command to make disciples?

Notes

[1]Leonard I. Sweet, *Soul Café*, vol. 3, no. 7–9, 15.

[2]Danny E. Morris and Charles M. Olsen, *Discerning God's Will Together* (Nashville: Upper Room Books, 1997), 92–93.

[3]Julia KuhnWallace, "Led by a Child," *Alive Now*, March/April, 1998 (Nashville: Upper Room), 22–23.

[4]L. Cecile Adams, "The Hallmark of Hospitality," *Alive Now*, March/April, 1998 (Nashville: Upper Room), 38.

[5]Stephen Ministries, 2045 Innerbelt Business Center Drive, St. Louis, MO 63114–5765; 314-428-2600.

[6]Pat Peterson, "A Litany of Reconciliation," *Alive Now*, March/April, 1994 (Nashville: Upper Room), 22–23.

[7]Leslie D. Weatherhead, *The Will of God* (Nashville: Abingdon Press, 1970), 14.

[8]Ibid., 24.

[9]Ibid., 38–39.

[10]Robin Karr-Morse and Meredith S. Wiley, *Ghosts from the Nursery: Tracing the Roots of Violence* (New York: The Atlantic Monthly Press,1997).

[11]Story used by permission of Godwin Hlatshwayo, citizen of Zimbabwe, who was a missionary in residence with the Common Global Ministries Board of Disciples of Christ and UCC, Cleveland, Ohio.

[12]Henri Nouwen, *Reaching Out* (New York: Doubleday, 1975), 72.

[13]Patterned after the closing worship service in the program "Stewardship of the Car," developed by Frankie Garrick and produced by the South Carolina United Methodist Conference, 1986.

[14]Malcolm Goldsmith, *Knowing Me Knowing God* (Nashville: Abingdon Press, 1997), 57.